Own It

Own It

The Power of Women at Work

Sallie Krawcheck

CROWN
BUSINESS
NEW YORK

Crown Business books are available at special discounts for bulk purchases for sales promotions or corporate use. Special editions, including personalized covers, excerpts of existing books, or books with corporate logos, can be created in large quantities for special needs. For more information, contact Premium Sales at (212) 572-2232 or e-mail specialmarkets@penguinrandomhouse.com.

Library of Congress Cataloging-in-Publication Data is available upon request.

ISBN 978-1-101-90625-5
eBook ISBN 978-1-101-90626-2

Printed in the United States of America

Jacket design by Tal Goretsky
Jacket photograph by Peter Yang

10 9 8 7 6 5 4 3 2 1

First Edition

In memory of my grandmother, who tore down a lot of walls. With thanks to my family, and particularly my amazing kids, supportive husband, and best friend brother.

Contents

Contents

My "Aha!" Moment

Well, here we are.

But the view looks a little different than we expected, right? After all, weren't we supposed to have arrived? Perhaps with our first female president, gender pay parity was in sight and workplace parity would come soon thereafter? Or, if that was asking too much, at least the end of "locker room talk"? And, if you're an optimist, weren't we going to be able to do this while also achieving the elusive work-life balance?

Well, not yet. Not so much.

The tough truth is that progress on gender diversity in corporate America (and elsewhere) has been slower than many expected, even with all of the research on how it helps business performance, and all of the advice telling professional women how to get ahead. Has feminism hit a plateau? Only if we continue to do the same things—and expect different results.

Luckily, there is another way. And that's why I am facing the future with real optimism. Because we can change this; we can own this.

As you'll read in the coming pages, my optimism is due, in large part, to the fact that the business world is changing—fast—

and it's changing in ways that play to our strengths. This places us on the brink of a seismic shift in the traditional power structure: one with significant implications for women in business. And it's a shift that begins with recognizing the power that we already have—and using that power to accelerate these changes.

So I'm not here to tell you how to win yesterday's version of the game, in which we women are instructed to develop some set of not-too-hot-and-not-too-cold skills for yesterday's world. And I'm not here to teach you yesterday's rules for achieving yesterday's version of success.

Nor am I here to "empower" you. Yes, you read that right. Because to be honest, I'm pretty over the whole notion of women being empowered. Look it up in the dictionary and you'll see why:

Empower (verb): to give power or authority to.

That's right, to empower women, power must be *given* to them. Well, this book isn't going to be about the slight sense of passivity that the definition implies. We shouldn't count on anyone else doing this for us.

Instead this book is going to be about how to take an *active* role in your future by owning the power you already have. I'm here to tell you that *you already have the qualities and skills it takes to get ahead in the modern workplace,* and, that in owning those qualities, you have more power and potential than you realize.

So rather than looking to be "empowered," this book is going to be about how to leverage our existing power to thrive and advance in our careers in ways that play to our strengths, how to turn our companies into places at which we want to work (or leave to start our own), and how to invest our economic muscle in making our lives and the world better.

Who am I to tell this story? Well, I've been around. I spent my career on Wall Street, starting out as a data-driven research analyst: I've run Smith Barney, at the time part of Citigroup, where I also served as chief financial officer. I've run Merrill Lynch Wealth Management, the "thundering herd." I've run U.S. Trust and the Citi Private Bank. I've led teams of more than thirty thousand financial advisors and bankers, and reported directly to CEOs of multibillion-dollar organizations. I've sat on a number of corporate boards. Today I chair Ellevate Network, the global professional women's network. And, most recently, I launched Ellevest, a digital investment platform for women, funded with venture capital money.

Two things have set me apart in all these settings. First: I've invariably been the only woman, or one of the only women, in the room.

Second: I've often been the only person to question the status quo. I've often been the lone voice saying, "Hold on a second. Slow down. Maybe we should talk this out before jumping in."

And I'm going to drop a bomblet here: I believe that those two things—my being a female and my approaching business differently from the others in the room—are related.

To understand this better, let's go back to Wall Street, circa 2008. Because it was there that capitalism broke—nearly taking the global economy down with it—and I had a front-row seat. It was also then that I was fired (on the front page of the *Wall Street Journal*, no less); because, when the economy imploded, I alone at the big Wall Street firms fought to do the unthinkable: reimburse some of our clients' investment losses.

I know. Crazy, right?

At Smith Barney, we had sold a set of investment products by the name of Falcon that were supposed to be low-risk. In a good market, the thinking went, their value would increase; in a down market, their value would drop, but not much. The downside was, we told our clients, maybe 8 cents on the dollar.

Well, as we all know too well, in 2007 and 2008 the market did go down—a lot. Falcon? It went down, too, but not 8 cents.

Not 15 cents or even 35 cents. It lost *most* of its cents on the dollar. Our team had misread the risk of the investment, and it had cost our clients dearly.

I was sick over it.

And so I approached my boss, the new CEO of Citigroup, with the position, unorthodox on Wall Street, that we should share some of the pain of the mistake—of *our* mistake—with our clients. I proposed giving them back some of the money that our miscalculation had cost them.*

My boss wouldn't even meet with me to discuss it. Instead he had one of his squad let me know that his answer was no—no way were we returning any of the money we had lost our clients. Not a cent of it.

Surely, I reasoned, he hadn't understood that we had made a mistake, which we should make right. So I tried again, appealing to him with a new analysis on how badly our clients had been hit as a result of costly miscalculations; he still said no.

I became obsessed, totally consumed with thinking about the clients whom we had let down. The clients whom we had built relationships with, who had trusted us to make the right investment decisions for them. And when I couldn't think about them anymore, I thought about the long-term harm that we were doing to our business. We had shaken those clients' confidence in us, so why would they ever want to invest their hard-earned dollars with us again?

I sent another analysis and another, and he said no again and again. The message I was sent was to "sit down and shut up."

I remember at one point during this back-and-forth—this

---

* Full disclosure: clients for the investment included any number of senior managers of the company and the board, including yours truly. My stance was that employees of the company should be left out of any reimbursement.

would be around the time the CEO stopped calling on me in executive committee meetings—thinking that if I took this one step further on, the *best* outcome would be that I would lose my job and we would return some of our clients' money. The more likely outcome was that we *wouldn't* return their money—and I would still lose my job.

I took one more step.

The board of directors of the company asked to be briefed on the debate. We met with them, played out the pros and cons, and they voted to partially reimburse the clients . . . and, no big surprise, within months my boss fired me—yep, I was out of the company and onto my backside. The company leaked the news to CNBC before it was finalized; I'll never forget watching it come across the tape from what would soon no longer be my office.

If you'd asked me in that moment, as I was putting framed photos of my kids into a cardboard box, if I'd been fired because I was a woman, I would have told you, *Absolutely not! That's ridiculous. It was a good old-fashioned business disagreement. How could you even imply such a thing?*

But now, as time has given me the distance and perspective—and the research analyst in me has replaced emotion with facts—I'd say, *Yes, in a way, I believe I was.* I know that's a horrifying statement. But you'll see my larger point in just a minute.

I don't mean I was fired because I had different body parts; I mean I was fired for being different, for challenging the majority opinion, for speaking up, for daring to go against the grain. I was fired for calling out the risk, prioritizing the long term, and for putting client relationships ahead of the short-term bottom line.

In other words, I was fired for some of the things that, the research you'll read about in subsequent chapters tells me, were driven . . . at least in some part . . . by my being female.

Maybe I was right in taking that stance; maybe I was wrong. One can certainly argue the point both ways. But what we *can't* argue is this: it would have been better for Wall Street to have had *more* of those kinds of disagreements, rather than *fewer* of them.

In the aftermath of my dismissal, some of the press predicted that the job offers would come flooding in for me, given my business track record and now pretty well proven client focus. But I had broken ranks with the industry, and the message was clear: I wasn't "one of them." So the phone *didn't* ring; the emails *didn't* come flooding in.

Okay, so what next? As a "recovering research analyst" with time on my hands, I spent that downtime (on the sofa, in sweatpants, often with a glass of wine handy) thinking through—what else?—the causes of the 2008 financial crisis, where this had all begun.

I thought and I thought. I dug through the reams of research, and then I dug some more. It seemed like my responsibility, given my front row seat on Wall Street and how much spare time I now had, to examine the issue from a number of angles.

So what did I conclude caused the crash? There is of course no single reason, or even a few reasons. And there are many theories: much of the press blamed the downturn on corporate greed. Let's concede the point that there is greed on Wall Street. But there is greed in other businesses as well, so that can't be the whole story.

Others chalk it up to dishonesty. They claim that the powers that be at the banks knew how much risk they were peddling to their clients and chose to deceive them about it. But if it was that simple, why did so many bankers actually seem to believe in what they were selling? Why did so many of them never sell *their own* shares of their companies' stocks when they started to tumble?

Other oft-cited reasons include too much financial leverage, the increased short-termism of business, and the mind-boggling complexity of these businesses. Yes to all.

But there's one more factor. Now, I have probably worked directly for more financial services CEOs than anyone else out there. Thus I have worked on more senior management teams than anyone else out there, and this is my take from what I saw: most of the people working in finance were not cartoon-character evil. (In all my years on Wall Street, I never witnessed a crime among them.) But they *were* people who had worked together for years, went to the same universities, sent their kids to the same schools, attended the same training programs, dined at the same restaurants, got promoted together, vacationed together, played tennis together, drank together, and sat on charitable boards together.

Therein lay the problem. The thinking converged. People approached decisions in the same way. Leadership teams imposed neither checks nor balances on one another. Individuals didn't fundamentally challenge one another. I saw any number of executives finish one another's sentences. As a result, Wall Street suffered from what I call the "false comfort of agreement."

As the 2008 economic crisis—as well as many crises of many stripes that came before it—shows us, it's not good for anyone when the people in charge all see things the same way. When you all have the same blind spot, you can wind up in some pretty epic accidents.

So my conclusion: the economy was felled not just by greed, stupidity, or even deliberate deception but, at its core, by a little discussed but insidious problem: groupthink.

And what's the antidote to groupthink?

Diversity. That means diversity of opinion. Diversity of perspective. Diversity of background. Diversity of disposition. Diversity of experience. Diversity of education. Diversity of orientation. Diversity of skin color.

And diversity of gender.

I know, I know . . . I know what you may be thinking. I can almost hear you. "I've got it," you're saying. "I understand gender diversity. I know a lot about women. After all, I work with women; I have a daughter; I have a mother; a sister; a cousin. Some of my best friends are women. Hell, I *am* a woman."

I, too, had a lot of strongly held views for a lot of years on the subject of women, and in particular on women in the workplace. And I'll admit, I wasn't always fully sold on the power of gender diversity. I didn't *not* believe in it; I just didn't think about it very much. I've never been a girly girl or a girl's girl. In fact, I was bullied right out of my all-girls middle school. I've traditionally gotten along better with guys ... and I really loved working with guys. The truth is, I like men, quite a bit. (Heck, I even married a couple of them.)

During my years in corporate America, I always believed in equality for women, but being a feminist wasn't one of the headlines I would use in describing myself. Nor did I particularly think of myself as a "female businessperson." When described as such, I bristled, and brushed off those inevitable questions of what it was like to be "a female in a male world." When people marveled at how I managed to have kids and work a tough job, I marveled at why no one ever said that about male corporate leaders.

But ...

I'm also a research analyst at heart. And to be a successful research analyst, you have to let the data speak to you. You know the saying: "Facts are stubborn things."

And the time I've spent looking at the facts has convinced me that women are ... you know ... *different* from guys.* It's true. Studies show that women are more empathetic. We are more risk aware. We take a more nuanced, long-term view when making decisions. We focus more on relationships, on people. Sound

---

* Yes, every woman is different, just as every man is different. And some fall way outside of the averages. But these averages exist nonetheless, and we should acknowledge and analyze them.

familiar? Yes, all those same qualities that drove me to return the clients' money—and subsequently got me booted from Wall Street—are qualities that can be inherently female.

And so, ironically, it was my getting fired that brought me to the epiphany—the "aha" moment—that, far from being a liability, our differences as women can be a *good* thing. A very good thing. And in fact, as you'll read later in the book, these differences are the very qualities that brought me to where I am today in my career: a place that is more fulfilling and has the potential to be more powerful, more impactful, and more badass than the biggest jobs I ever held on Wall Street.

So, yes, we women are different. *And therein lie our greatest strength and competitive advantage in the modern workplace.*

The flip side of groupthink is greater diversity. I'll take you through some of the troves of research on the positive business results that derive from gender diversity for companies. But I would further argue that our businesses and economy don't just need more women in the workplace and in leadership positions and starting businesses (though we do). We need more women *acting more* like women. And this goes not just for female CEOs or women in top senior leadership positions, but for all women.

That's because the power of diversity is . . . wait for it . . . *diversity.*

What I mean is that the real power of diversity comes not by hiring a bunch of women (or any other group) and teaching them, training them, coaching them to be men-like creatures: asking for the raise like men, showing decisiveness like men, negotiating like men. It's us women (and other groups) embracing and doubling down on the power of our diversity. It's us women deciding to celebrate rather than apologize for all the amazing unique qualities that we bring to the table—and to give ourselves permission to act like our true selves at work. So why does so much of the advice out there today have us conform, rather than own our differences?

Not convinced about the power of diversity? Here's one way to think about it: What if we pulled together a group of alumni from the University of North Carolina's men's basketball team?* Some of the greats. And of that group, we chose the five best. What if those five were Phil Ford, Ty Lawson, Raymond Felton, Jimmy Black, and Kendall Marshall. (Side note: Michael Jordan was busy somewhere else that day . . . because he's Michael Jordan.) Those are five terrific players. But put them on a team together and would they win a national basketball championship?

No.

Why? Because they're all point guards.

Now, the point guard is arguably the most important player on the team; after all, the point guard runs the plays. The point guard brings the ball down the court. The point guard is the natural team leader. But you can't win a national championship with all point guards. You can't have five guys trying to run the plays. You need the other members of the team—with all their diverse skills—working together. You need—here comes that word again—diversity. True diversity.

So, how can we leverage this power we hold—the power of our diverse skills and strengths—while recognizing that sexism, whether subtle or not so subtle, and gender stereotypes still exist, even among us women? How do we tap into and even amplify power and potential that we have. How do we play our own game by our rules, and play it to win?

No one has ever accused me of being a Pollyanna. Recent events have shown that the progress of feminism is not an inevitable, inexorable straight line. In order for the future to be different we must act differently. We have the power to accelerate change in the world.

---

* I'm a Tar Heel. And a rabid basketball fan. Beware my Twitter feed during basketball season.

While our career choices even a handful of years ago were limited ("Hmm, I'm not happy at XYZ Company; maybe I'll take a job at ABC Company, which I don't know that much about, or stay at home"), today professional women have more choices than ever. We have growing amounts of information and greater transparency into our own companies, and to companies we might want to work for. More of us are choosing nontraditional careers, and more of us are finding that starting our own business is now within reach. At the same time, more of us are finding networks and virtual networks that inform and support us as we work through evaluating and navigating these increasing options and career transitions. You'll also see how we have more financial and economic power than we know—and that using it and growing it can accelerate this change.

Today I'm the CEO and cofounder of Ellevest, a digital investment platform for women. I couldn't have started this company even a handful of years ago; the costs would have been too high, and the technology wasn't available. But the changes that are happening in business today have allowed me to start a company that can have a real impact (in this case, on women by closing the gender investing gap), a company with a culture that requires excellence but embraces difference. Starting your own business isn't for everyone, but the changes that are afoot mean that many more have greater opportunities to build fulfilling careers for ourselves in whatever traditional or nontraditional ways that make sense for us.

So we can't control everything. But we can own this.

Women already make the companies at which they work better—we'll spend some time talking about how. But here's the thing: not only is the world of business changing, rapidly; *it's changing in ways that make us women more valuable assets to our companies and employees than ever.* That's because those same forces that are increasing our career options and potential career

11

paths (think greater transparency into our companies, as well as increased opportunities to forge nontraditional careers) are unleashing enormous and unprecedented power for women.

This book is about how each one of us can own that power and, in doing so, take control not only of our own destinies, but also of the larger narrative about women at work. And let's be very clear: this is not about *excluding* men. It's about *including* women. We have the power to show the world that more women at the table is good for women *and* men. It's good for companies *and* families. It's good for the economy *and* it's good for society as a whole.

I've written this book as a means of sharing what I've learned about all of this, both on the front lines of the biggest boys' club in the world and now as an entrepreneur. I have written it to show how we can recognize and leverage the growing power we hold as women to go beyond just snagging a seat at the table, and instead truly take our careers and the business world to the next level.

As you'll read in the chapters that follow, despite the inevitable setbacks, we women are on the brink of an extraordinary rise. The future is ours to seize. But we aren't going to seize it by contorting ourselves into the male version of what power and success look like or continuing to do exactly what we've done to date. Instead we're going to do it by embracing and investing in our true female selves—and bringing those badass selves proudly, unapologetically, to work.

PART I

The Future of Work . . . and How We Can Own It

CHAPTER 1

How the World of Work Is Changing— and Why That's Good News for Women

Ask for the raise. Negotiate like a man, but not too much like a man. Be helpful in the office, but don't become the work wife. But do find a work husband. Use silence as a tool. Speak up. But don't up-speak. Lower your voice to be really heard. Develop the all-important gravitas. Be forceful, but not too forceful, or you won't be likable. Dress like your boss.

The advice out there for women in the workplace is dizzying, and I haven't even gotten to the whole work-life balance debate: *We can have it all! Oh no, wait, we can't? Well, maybe we can, but only if we don't expect to have it all at once . . . or if we marry just the right person . . . or if we have our kids early . . . or later . . . but not too late. . . .*

It all boils down to the same advice: "Change." And even "Act more like . . . you know . . . a man."

It's exhausting.

It can't be denied that, to quote the great Loretta Lynn, we've come a long way, baby. I'm proof positive of that. In my grandmothers'—and even my mother's—generation, a woman like me at the senior levels of Wall Street, the ultimate boys' club, holding top jobs at some of the biggest financial firms on the planet, and now founding my own digital investment start-up, El-levest, would have been unheard of.

But here's the thing. Contrary to conventional wisdom, I didn't do it by following the old rules. I didn't do it by trying to "act like a man," or "beat them at their own game." I didn't do it "in spite of" being a woman.

With hindsight I can see that I did it *because* I'm a woman, because I embraced and invested in the powerful and unique strengths that, research shows, can make women valuable employees, terrific team players, and effective leaders. And because I brought those qualities—unabashedly and unapologetically—to work.

Did I encounter my share of sexism along the way? You know it, and you'll read some of these harrowing stories in this book. (For example, in the early days of my career, every day began with me finding a photocopy of a penis on my desk. Every day. Bright side: I managed to keep in shape by using the stairs to do all of my copying on a different floor.)

And was my career a straight line? Absolutely not. I'll talk about how holding true to those same qualities meant that I also had some real—and public—career setbacks, but I'll also talk about how those same qualities helped me bounce back from them, and even move my career further forward in the process.

Has my success as a woman in a man's world been, in many ways, the exception rather than the rule? You can bet your bottom dollar on that, too. When I worked on senior management teams on Wall Street, there was rarely a time when I wasn't the only woman—or one of only a couple of women—in the room. Still today, just 4 percent of Fortune 500 CEOs are women,[1] and women make up less than 19 percent of the members of corporate boards.[2] There are literally more men named John, Robert, William, or James on corporate boards than there are women.[3] And when women *do* move into senior business roles, it's still so rare—so utterly astounding—that it garners press attention, always with the tired, but inevitable, questions about work-life balance, how does she do it . . . and, too often, the even more insulting question of what is she wearing while she's doing it.

What's more, we women still earn just 78 cents on men's dollar—52–64 cents if we are women of color.[4] At this rate, we won't reach gender pay parity until 2133.[5] Professional women overwhelmingly report that gender discrimination still exists at their companies: some 63 percent say it is subtle and 26 percent say it's overt.[6] And after all of our hard work, we women do not invest our earnings into the markets to the same extent men do; depending on our income, this can cost us literally hundreds of thousands, or even millions, of dollars over the course of our lifetimes. All of this can leave us financially dependent—on men.

We've come a long way, baby. But some things are still a little 1958.

If our economy were humming along, we might sigh and dismiss all this as a "feminist issue." But we don't have the luxury of throwing up our hands and declaring it something for the Gloria Steinems of the next generations to sort out. The fact is that the gender gap in business and in investing has coincided with chronic underemployment, sluggish economic growth, the retirement savings crisis, growing income inequality, and fear for the future of the middle class.

But this is all ripe for change, and that change can come fast.

I would go so far as to say that we are at a major turning point in the role of women at work. The role of women is on the brink of change because the world of business is on the brink of change—the kind of change, as you'll read in the pages ahead, that gives us more power in the workforce than ever.

So what is driving this change? And why can it happen now?

I believe there are four key catalysts.

1. The Increasing Recognition of What We Women Bring to the Party

For years, as I said earlier, I sort of fought the idea that women are "different" from men. . . . Hey, we're all just people, and each of us is unique. I always resisted the notion that either gender—men or women—might possess inherent qualities that made it inherently "different" or "better" at business than the other. But as a "recovering research analyst," I always try to let the research speak to me, and when I began to drill down on these issues, what I found surprised me. The research shows that women *do* bring "different" traits to the office that are good for business. Okay, even great for business. Among them: advanced risk awareness; a holistic perspective and ability to juggle complexity and multitask; long-term thinking; a focus on relationships and team building; a love of lifelong learning; and acute awareness of meaning, purpose, and social impact.

We'll spend time on each of these traits in Chapter 2, where we'll talk about the evidence showing how these traits can make us, to put it bluntly, pretty awesome: awesome leaders, awesome team members, and awesome employees. And why that in turn means that more women, and particularly more women in leadership positions, make those more diverse companies more innovative, more profitable, and better places to work.

Think I'm exaggerating?

Study after study shows that the companies with greater gender diversity outperform others on many measures. These include: Improved financial performance, in some cases dramatically better performance, with higher returns on investment, lower risk, narrower gender pay gaps, greater long-term focus, and lower cost of borrowing.[7] Better customer service and better public image.[8] Increased ability to attract the best talent.[9] More creative and effective decision making. The power of diversity is so great that more diverse teams outperform "smarter" ones.[10] (Okay, wow.)

Benefits also include: Higher worker engagement and better morale.[11] (This is a biggie.) Increased innovation.[12] (Yes, you read that correctly.) Better stockholder returns.[13] (You read that one correctly, too. And that's not just true over time, but is recognized pretty quickly by the market.) And if your company is a start-up, the benefits of diversity exist there, too. Again, not by a little: one source reports 63 percent better investment performance from companies with a female founder.[14]

The research is loud and clear: a company with women in leadership positions is healthier on every level, and can bring out the best in everyone.

The fact that this research exists in the first place is a sign of the growing recognition of the power of women in the workplace and in the economy and reflects an emerging understanding of the qualities we women bring to the party. It's evidence that the view that closing the gender gaps at work can be good for everybody (not just women themselves) is beginning to take hold.

So this is good.

But is this recognition enough to drive real change? Is it enough to convince those already in power to work to toss aside whatever gender stereotypes or misconceptions they adhere to (you know, such as that women aren't "tough enough" to succeed in the cut-throat, high-rung world of business, or are "too emotional" to make strong leaders)? Is it enough to persuade them to further open the doors for people who are not a lot like them? Is it enough to convince the boss to promote Susie instead of Jimmy (even though Jimmy reminds him so darn much of himself when he was younger . . .) in pursuit of the positive ripple effects of diversity?

Maybe.

But also maybe not.

And it may not matter. Because here's what else is different going forward.

2. The Business World Is Rapidly Changing . . . and So Are the Drivers of Success—in a Way That Makes the Skills We Women Bring to the Workplace More Valuable than Ever

I don't think it's controversial to say that technology is fundamentally changing the workplace as we know it.

Remember when gathering information was costly and took forever? Remember when the only ways to engage with the customer at scale were through magazines, newspapers, and broadcast TV? Remember when you could dictate to the customer, and they had no way to talk back?

Well, all of that has changed, and the pace of further change is only increasing. Success at work now is less about having and hoarding information and more about the ability to analyze and synthesize that information with acuity. It's less about simply building the best product and hoping for the money to follow and more about building the kinds of relationships with customers that sustain profits over the long term. Business is more complex, and so it requires the ability to make and understand connections, the ability to see the forest through the trees.

The ability to see problems holistically, emotional intelligence, communication—things we females can be awfully good at—thus matter more every day. So the workplace is changing in ways that, research shows, play to women's innate skills. And in turn the more that we invest in these skills—skills like empathy, love of learning, and acute awareness of purpose—the better positioned we can be to succeed.

But that's not all.

3. Technology Is Also Increasing Our Career Options . . . and Thus Increasing Our Power

When I ran Merrill Lynch, we had in place an investment platform (the most whiz-bang, the most advanced one in the industry) that cost more than $1 billion to build.

Today I run Ellevest. We have built an investment platform that doesn't have all the bells and whistles of Merrill's, and uses as much third-party software as possible as its building blocks, but accomplishes the same fundamental functions—at a tiny fraction of what Merrill spent to put its platform in place. Teeny tiny.

This is but one example of how, thanks to technology, all kinds of barriers to starting businesses are coming down—and fast. As recently as five years ago, if you wanted to start a business, you had to rent long-term office space, buy expensive servers, hire coders and programmers, figure out how to put in place HR systems, and so on. Today you can store information in the cloud, hire freelancers, and rent short-term space at a WeWork, all for a fraction of the cost. While venture capitalists don't "get it" on women (and particularly women of color), the sources of capital for starting businesses are expanding—think crowdfunding and angel investing groups. So while it's by no means *easy* to start a business (trust me on this), it is *easier*, and cheaper.

That is why more and more people—and more and more women—can leave the more traditional, corporate career path behind for the world of entrepreneurship. Just look at the businesses that are being built by women, like Jessica Herrin at Stella and Dot, Julie Wainwright at The RealReal, Jennifer Hyman at Rent the Runway, Alli Webb at Drybar, and many, many more. So not only do we now have the tools to make the plunge into entrepreneurship easier and are able to start businesses more easily; we're also getting a critical mass of role models who are making this career path feel more attainable than ever.

Thus, it may be no wonder that women are now starting businesses at double the rate of men.[15] (And the bonus is that a good number of these businesses are themselves focused on the female customer, making our lives better and, in some cases, more fun.)

I get that throwing yourself whole hog into starting your own business isn't for everyone nor does everyone have the financial resources to do so. But today's technology also offers us an intermediate step, since these same tools are also enabling the explosion of flexible and part-time work, to the point that these forms of employment have become true career paths; and these can be ones that can coexist with the demands of family in a way that many full-time corporate jobs still don't.

It's been said again and again that we are entering a great age of entrepreneurialism. I would argue that the truth is even more exciting than that: I would argue that we are actually entering a great age of *female entrepreneurialism.* And this provides women with more options—and in turn, more power—than ever before.

At the same time, technology enables us to know more about our employers—everything from their approach to diversity to their corporate culture to, increasingly, exactly how much they pay men versus women for the same job or role—at the click of a mouse. (Think sites like Fairygodboss, Glassdoor, The Muse, Hired.com, and Comparably.)

This access to information enables us to hold our companies more accountable than ever for how they treat their employees and what their diversity policies are, in a way that simply wasn't possible even a few years ago.

Taken together, what this all means is that if our employers aren't serving our needs—if they aren't valuing us, aren't promoting us, don't have family-friendly policies in place—we can know that and leave them for another company that does the woman thing better. Or we can start our own companies and do the culture thing even better still.

Thus, these changes in business mean we have leverage. We have options. And our options are more varied and more exciting than ever.

But there's one more thing.

4. We Have Economic Power—More Than We Know

Women today make up just more than half of the workforce. We make 80 percent of consumer purchases.[16] We control $5 trillion of investable assets in the United States alone. We jointly control another $6 trillion with our partners and spouses.[17] And, given our longer lives, we stand to inherit some $29 trillion in the coming decades.[18]

I'm not the first to say it: money is power. And we have more of it than ever.

And we are increasingly able to use that power, in part, once again, because of technology, to effect change on an unprecedented scale. I spoke earlier about how we can know so much more about the companies we work for. Technology is similarly granting us access to information on the companies we buy from or invest in, and social media is providing us with the means to share that information much more broadly and, if we choose to, organize ourselves around issues we care about. So now not only can we choose not to work for a company that isn't serving women well; we can choose to stop buying from it (check out BuyUp) or investing in it. And we can encourage others to do so as well.

Thus, we no longer have no choice but to wait for the world to go our way. Today we have the tools and the leverage to create the progress we want in our careers, our workplaces, and society at large.

And I would note that this isn't just good for us as women. What happens at the macro level, to the economy, when women are more fully engaged, both professionally and financially?

Yet more great things: The economy grows. By a lot. McKinsey estimates that fully engaging women in the economy can add $12 trillion in economic growth.[19] Now that's a wow. The retirement savings gap shrinks. (That's because the gender earnings and investing gaps and the retirement savings gap are inextricably linked.)[20] Our global economic competitiveness increases.[21] We arguably become better insulated from the devastation of future financial crises.[22] And even our families are better off,[23] and particularly our daughters: the daughters of working mothers earn 23 percent more later in life than those whose mothers stayed home.[24]

So let's recap. We women bring valuable skills to work today, and those skills are becoming even more valuable as the world changes. At the same time, our career options are expanding and we have massive amounts of financial power.

Valuable skills + more career options + more information + financial power. What does that equal? The opportunity to have an impact. A big impact.

But it's not just enough to hold that power. We need to own that power and put it to work. And that can't happen until we throw out the old playbook and stop buying into the dogma that to succeed in business we need to play by the men's rules or operate within the walls of the box as they exist today. We can move the walls, and play by our own rules, and, in doing so, we can drive massive positive change in the workplace and society in a way that wasn't possible even a handful of years ago.

Smart companies will get this and prosper. They will reap the benefits of women's skill sets and energy as the world evolves into a place in which those skills are more valued than ever. They will benefit from stronger leadership, a more engaged and productive workforce, and more innovation. If the research is right (and it is), these companies' performance will be superior, which will generate profitability to invest back into their businesses, which will in turn enable them to grow more, providing more profits to invest, and so on. At the same time, some number of us will look to spend our money at, and invest our money in, companies that "get it" as well, so there will be a further ripple effect. And this will open up unprecedented opportunities for women. A virtuous circle, if I ever saw one.

And what about companies that don't get this? Companies that continue to do business 1980s-style will suffer the reverse effects as at an unprecedented rate we women flee to work at companies that "get it"—or start our own. (Think that paying women less has no cost? Today, more women in their thirties leave their jobs for higher salaries than men do—65 percent versus 56 percent—according to an ICEDR study. And this will only increase as salary transparency increases.)

Sure, for now we may still have to fight for the promotions and the raises (big sigh . . .), but smart companies are beginning to figure out that we deserve the raise not because it's the fair or the right thing to do (though it is) but because we bring qualities to work that make our companies more innovative, our bottom lines stronger, and our workplaces better.

How women are treated at work is not just a moral issue or a social issue—it's a business and economic one. That's a big part of why I bought the professional women's network Ellevate as a means for women to take action to help themselves—and other women—move ahead.

That's also why I decided to go even deeper with this whole entrepreneurship thing by starting my investment company, Ellevest. I saw a real need to engage women more fully not just in their careers, but also in their finances, and I saw that traditional (mostly male) Wall Street was not meeting that need. My team and I are working to build a business around the way *women* want to engage with their money, instead of forcing us to "invest like a man." (I mean, have you ever seen an industry with as many war and sports analogies than the investing industry, with all the talk of "Beat the market," "outperform," "pick the winners"? And the industry symbol is a bull. I rest my case.) As a result, we women are not investing our money to the same extent as men are; and we can end up with as much as a third less in assets than men over the course of our lives.

I believe strongly in the mission of both companies. And I believe we're at a tipping point of women's engagement in the workplace, and the economy. But to tip these scales we need to commit to making a real and sustained investment into owning the leadership power and potential of women.

So the goal of this book is to show that being a woman in the business world is something to embrace and celebrate, not something to overcome or hide. This book will show that being a woman in the business world is not a *liability;* it's *power.* And it will provide a practical roadmap for how to position yourself for these changes from a place of strength. This will involve tapping into and even amplifying that power to get you to where you want to go in your career, not by contorting yourself to the demands of today's (still more male-friendly) workplace, but by bringing your innate strengths to work and positively impacting the workplace of tomorrow.

In this book, we'll talk about how we hold the power to raise ourselves up professionally and lift the glass ceiling in the process—by playing to our strengths, by investing in those qualities that define us, by doubling down on our innate skills (rather than trying to "fix" ourselves all the time), and by recognizing how much economic power we already have. We'll talk about how by owning our diversity, we women can do better for our families, our economy, and our society, and we can make a world where our daughters and daughters' daughters can succeed not in spite of being female, but because of it.

We can create these changes and with them enormous and unprecedented opportunities for us all. I would even go so far as to say we are in a new age of feminism. Why?

Because there is a yet unwritten chapter to the evolving story of women's equality, and that's the issue of women and money. I believe that in a capitalist society it is only through achieving full economic engagement—and thus full equality over our money—that we women will achieve full equality. In other words, women will not be fully equal with men until we are financially equal with men.

Just as the first waves of feminism made for a richer, more diverse, more inclusive society, so, too, this will filter up into a more vibrant, more diverse, less risky economy. It will mean higher-performing, more resilient companies. It will mean more family-friendly work policies. It will mean more financially secure families. It will mean greater innovation. It will mean greater opportunities for women in business, and for all women.

So how do we get there? That's what this book is all about.

Getting from Here to There

The first step is to realize that we have the ability to own that power in the first place. Let's give ourselves permission to acknowledge that we hold a pretty great hand of cards here. Remember those attributes I listed? And the positive impact we have on businesses and on profits? These are real, and they are game-changing.

In Part I of this book, I'll discuss the qualities that we bring and how they make us well positioned for success in business and leadership, qualities like risk awareness, relationship skills, ability to manage complexity, and more. I'll share some stories from my career—both building a business and from my time on Wall

Street (you're not going to believe some of these Wall Street stories, but I promise you they all happened)—to demonstrate how investing and doubling down on my strengths helped me succeed; again, it was not *despite* my "femaleness," but *because* of it. And I'll show how they can help you as well.

In Part II we'll turn to the concrete actions we can all take to capitalize on and own the rapid shifts in the business world to further our careers, no matter what industry we're in, or what stage we are at in our careers. Most of these tips will draw on lessons that I've learned the hard way. (I always seem to learn them the hard way....) And I hope they'll prevent you from repeating my mistakes.

And, no, this won't require a ton of work. We're already doing most of the hard work (at ... you know ... work). Nor will it require you to change. Simply adding a few tools to our tool chest—the kind that play to our existing strengths—will provide outsize impact for us all.

That's why along the way we'll completely overturn some of the advice you've read in other "how to succeed in business as a woman" books crowding the shelves. To be clear, I do not believe that all that advice—that is, play the game the men's way—out there is "wrong"; what I *do* believe is that it is rapidly becoming outdated. There's no question that this advice got us to where we are, but if we want to truly go the distance, to close these significant gaps that still exist, we need a new way.

Also in Part II we'll look at some old saws like networking and mentoring, how to give and get feedback, and how to ask for that ever-important raise—but we'll look through a new lens. And since we're overturning the old rules and writing them anew, we'll need to embrace discomfort and a certain willingness to fail. We'll also talk about how to navigate—and make the most of—the career curveballs that will inevitably get hurled your way, all while learning to get over your fear of that F-word: *failure.*

And we'll discuss some of the best career advice out there that no one is talking about, and why getting in control of our finances is the key to achieving true flexibility and freedom in our careers.

In Part III we'll broaden the conversation to how we can affect changes in our workplaces. We'll hold a funeral for all the earnest but misguided approaches to gender equality and diversity that some companies keep rolling out, even though many ceased working some time ago. We'll talk about investing some of our hard-earned political capital in what the forward-thinking Ellyn Shook (head of HR at Accenture) has termed the "courageous conversations" that shape our companies into places we want to work: conversations on topics like diversity, flexibility without shame, and the kind of micro-sexism that can quickly seep into and infect an otherwise open and diverse workplace.

When done the right way, owning these conversations allows us to shape our companies into places we want to work.

Finally, in Part IV, we'll talk about paying it forward: making a big investment in your daughters' and granddaughters' futures. We'll look at how we can work to leverage our economic power, investing our hard-earned money and the influence that goes with it in the causes and companies we believe in.

Along the way, we'll own the solutions for some big problems: we'll even talk about how stepping into our economic power can close the retirement savings gap—you know, the one that is so big (up to $14 trillion in size[25]) and the solutions for which are so ugly (think tax increases and entitlement cuts), we've all but stopped talking about it in this country.

"Huh," you might be saying. "What is a discussion about the retirement savings gap doing in this book?" Well, as it happens, the retirement savings crisis affects mostly women—after all, we live an average of five+ years longer than men[26] and, also sadly, retire with two-thirds the money that men have, on average.[27] And this gender perspective changes everything. That's because if you recognize the crisis as a women's crisis, the possible solutions go from all negative to pretty much all positive. The path to closing the retirement savings gap ceases being about increasing taxes and reducing entitlements (ugh) and instead becomes about keeping women in the workforce longer, closing the gender pay gap, and closing the gender investing gap. If women are in the workforce longer and earning more, they're contributing to Social Security and their 401(k)s, helping to set themselves up for a more prosperous retirement. And these actions also have the impact of actually *growing* the economy, as more earnings means more economic activity and more investing means more capital for businesses to grow. Looking at this problem through the lens of gender (while it may feel uncomfortable at first) leads to a series of win-win-win solutions for us women and for the country as a whole.

Finally, a book like this wouldn't be complete without some thoughts on our home lives, too. Instead of taking sides on the endlessly debated (and in my opinion, beyond tired) question of whether women can "have it all," we'll talk about the question I strongly believe we should be asking instead: How can we be the kind of role models that our children can look up to? The kind that inspire our children to act with a combination of integrity and grit; that teach them that they, too, have the ability to both elevate themselves *and* change the world for the better, by owning the power of diversity and investing in themselves as they really are, rather than trying to be something else?

I'll also talk about how, when the going gets tough, you just gotta laugh. Because if I've learned anything from all of this, it's that if you can't keep your sense of perspective, your sense of humor, you're doomed. After all, we're all very fortunate to have the opportunity to work in these jobs, to have these conversations, to have this kind of impact. What's the point of working our tails off if we're miserable at the end of the day?

One final note: This book is written from my experience and

from my perspective. As a result, this is a book by and largely for professional women. This is my story. I recognize that there are so many working women who have not had the same choices I have been fortunate enough to have. I believe that as professional women are more successful, this gives us the power to improve not just our own lives, but to also have a positive impact on all women, collectively, and on society as a whole.

Ladies, companies, the economy, and society at large—they need us badly. And only once we get comfortable owning who we really are can we seize the great opportunities in front of us today and the even better ones it will open up for us tomorrow.

The world can go the women's way.

We have more power than we know.

As soon as we own our power, the future belongs to us.

CHAPTER 2

Six Things We Have Going for Us

Every day, I recognize how fortunate I am to have been born into a family that encouraged each of us to work hard and achieve.

My parents married young, struggled to establish themselves, and had four children quickly. (Age difference between oldest and youngest: three years and eleven months. No twins. Yes, it is mathematically possible.)

Early on, they went into debt to pay for our educations. They took on loans year after year after year . . . for us. It hurt, but they did it because they knew that with an education we had the opportunity to accomplish anything we wanted. With no limits. And there was never any question of whether my sister and I could achieve as much as our brothers, or whether we could achieve it while being ourselves, including being feminine.

I think a lot about something my dad once said to me. I was in fifth grade and had just gotten my first pair of glasses. They were Coke-bottle thick and tinted yellow (hey, it was the *Mod Squad* era). I fought hard against getting them, even resorting to such measures as moving to the first row in class to better see the blackboard and making my sister take the eye exam before me, so I could try to memorize the letters first. (Of course, in retrospect

I'm not sure why I was so resistant. The glasses complemented my braces, my freckles, and my center-parted Dorothy Hamill haircut perfectly.)

I came home crying from my first day of school wearing my new glasses. I remember my father asking me why I was upset. I told him that I didn't want to have to wear them.

"But I have glasses, too," he said.

"No, you don't understand," I told him. "I want to be pretty."

His response: "Sallie, you *are* pretty. And look at Gloria Steinem. She wears glasses, she's a knockout, and she's changing the world."

Here's what I took away:

- My father thought a woman could be both pretty and smart.
- He thought a woman could make a difference (worth noting, in 1970s South Carolina).
- This Gloria Steinem woman was changing the world. And she wore glasses. And my dad clearly approved.

In doing this, he pointed me toward a role model, and made me feel appreciated and that I could be *myself*, tinted glasses and all. Research indeed shows that one of the most important relationships in determining a woman's success in the workplace is the one with her father; his support gives her confidence.[1] That was certainly true for me; if the most important man in my life believed in me, and believed I could succeed by being me—and that "me" was a girl—then I could certainly believe in myself.

I was also fortunate to find similar support in the workplace early on.

My first research job was at Sanford Bernstein; the director of research there made me an offer when no one else on Wall Street would. (Okay, one other firm did, but they withdrew it when they found out I had a baby at home. My startled reaction: "You wouldn't do this to a man, would you?" His startled response: "Of course not!")

I used to affectionately call Bernstein the "land of the misfit toys," since we weren't a group of Ivy League–educated, typical Wall Street types. Everyone was fiercely intelligent, but none had the traditional background you would expect to find at a Wall Street firm. One of the partners, for example, had driven a taxi immediately before starting there. The firm actively looked for a certain degree of scrappiness (and even insecurity) in the individuals it hired. Thus almost everyone there could best be described as having a "fighting spirit."

I received my first big promotion at Bernstein when I was visibly, heavily pregnant with my daughter. I was so surprised by the offer that I helpfully pointed out my condition (as if someone could miss it), but received only a shrug in return.

Bernstein didn't just challenge the status quo in their approach to hiring; they encouraged us to challenge the status quo in our research. If we didn't have anything different to say, the thinking went, what was the point of publishing it? When the CEO of one company I covered didn't like what I'd published and demanded that my boss "talk to me" about it (meaning, tell me to write only nice things), he did talk to me. But instead of reprimanding me, he said, "I promised I would have this meeting with you, so I am. But keep doing what you're doing. The fact that he's upset tells me you're onto something."

That meant I didn't have to show up at work every day acting like someone I wasn't. Since I didn't have to waste time, energy, and emotion in playing a part, I could think more clearly, "play looser," and learn more. I could operate in a state of "career flow."

Contrast that with another company I worked at later on, whose CEO did not like to have his perspective challenged. There I quickly learned that I had to take the temperature of the room before I spoke for fear of ruffling his feathers. *Wow*, I thought often. *I really don't know how to act. I don't know what to say.* It was that feeling of *I don't speak the language and everyone else is fluent.*

At which company do you think I was more effective, not to mention happier—the one where I could be myself, or the one where I had to size up the room every time I spoke? The one where I felt comfortable, was confident that I could be heard, or the one where my stress level rose every time I opened my mouth?

It was in comparing my comfort at these two very different companies that I began to believe that recognizing the strengths every individual brings to the table, and allowing them to play to those strengths, might be a more successful personnel strategy than training everyone to act the same way. That was around the time I also began to believe that allowing us women to act like ourselves in the workplace, to own and double down on those strengths, rather than downplay them, could be more effective, too.

So what *are* the strengths women bring to the table? In this chapter I'll distill the results of the dozens of studies showing that women possess six distinct strengths that can make our companies stronger, more profitable, and in turn better places for us to work: a healthy risk awareness, the ability to see things holistically (and thus manage complexity), our relationship focus, a longer-term perspective, a love of learning, and a drive for impact and meaning. In the sections ahead I'll talk not only about the power of each trait in business but also about how each of us can own and capitalize on that power in order to advance our careers.

A request is that we don't then interpret any of this as "women are better than men" or "men are better than women." Pointing out what we women bring to the party in a positive light isn't meant to be a negative against men. It's simply acknowledging the fact that the power of diversity is diversity . . . and that women bring to the table diverse strengths that provide a critical balance for the skills possessed by the men around them.

Trait #1: Risk-Averse, or Risk-Aware? Why Women's Looking Around Corners Is Just What Business Needs

Imagine a typical Wall Street trading floor. You're imagining a sea of white men in suits, right? Now imagine that same floor populated by a diverse mix of men and women.

Earlier I mentioned how, after examining the causes of the financial crisis from every angle, I concluded that if Wall Street had looked more like the country did in the years leading up to 2008—that is, if all the big Wall Street banks had had more diversity (and more women)—the financial crisis would have been much less severe.

This is not just my theory. In fact, it's what the data indicates. Research shows that asset bubbles like what we saw in the run-up to the market crash of 2007–08 are greater in markets in which there is homogeneity.[2] One theory is that in a market in which everyone looks the same, there's more inherent trust. More trust leads to more comfort and more blind agreement. It makes people question one another less. It means less "Excuse me, may I review those numbers?" and more "Hey, everyone, let's grab some beers!"

This type of easy camaraderie can lead to overconfidence, which leads to more errors, in large part because when there is no diversity, when everyone is thinking the same way, it can be tough to focus on risk. Nobody likes a naysayer or a party pooper, after all, when everyone else is in happy agreement.

I encountered this resistance at my very first Wall Street research job, at Sanford Bernstein. I remember being told just a couple of months in, in a fatherly tone, "Sallie, you're about to make the mistake that will end your career before it has even started."

This bombshell came from a senior executive at American General, a life insurance company. This was the same guy who had wholeheartedly welcomed me to the equity research industry a couple of months earlier, noting that we both had family roots in Charleston, South Carolina.

I had just sent him a draft of the very first equity research report I had ever written, for fact checking. I was a new life insurance associate (not even an analyst, but a more junior associate) and wet behind the ears. For my first assignment, I had dug into American General's growing subprime lending business. (This was before the word *subprime* was even really used.) The company had diversified into subprime lending to drive greater growth than was available in the ho-hum, traditional life insurance field.

While the world at large saw massive growth, by pulling apart the credit ratios I believed I saw a swiftly deteriorating credit picture that was being masked by that growth. And no, this wasn't 2007; it was 1994. The title of my report: "Whoa, Nelly." (What can I say? I'm from the South.)

The American General executive told me that my analysis was unconventional at best, not to mention obviously wrong, and a huge departure from the consensus view of analysts who had been in the business for years and years. The other analysts were focused on growth; why was I so focused on risk? Given all this, he asked, why would I be so foolish as to publish the research?

It reminded me of advice I once received from a successful analyst at one of the big Wall Street firms when I was first embarking on my career. This analyst had told me to be careful of making bearish—careful, "whoa Nelly"–like—calls. If you make a bullish call on a company's stock and you're right, I was told, all is good. You're a hero. Everyone loves an optimist. (They are so much more pleasant to be around, right?)

Bullish and wrong? Oh well. No harm, no foul. It could happen to anyone.

Bearish and right? The most you get is grudging respect.

But if you make a bearish call and you're wrong, he told me, you're done. Fired. Out. Done.

This analyst went on to inform me that Wall Street was the only industry in the world in which one could make millions of dollars by being mediocre and essentially hiding in the pack. One would be a fool to stand out as a Debbie Downer.

In other words, if I wanted to make it as an analyst, I needed to focus on the upside, not the risk.

As I listened to this American General executive, I was sweating out of every pore in my body—even pores I didn't know I had. Yet though I couldn't really articulate why at the time, I published that negative research anyway, without changing a single word. (I have recently taken some business personality tests that indicate I'm "disagreeable," so maybe that's the answer.)

It wasn't really that I was so sure the research was right—after all, I was brand-new to the industry and if the senior analysts weren't seeing what I thought I saw, who was I to be so sure? It was more because I had noticed the risk—the proof was sitting there, as clear as a bell to me—and found it puzzling that it wasn't being discussed. And, whether I was right or wrong, I felt like I needed to make investors aware of that risk, particularly if it was one others weren't talking about.

As it turned out, my research was right. When the company reported its next set of earnings, its credit deterioration was clearer—and, in fact, even worse than I had projected.

The thing is, this type of willful blindness to risk was not an isolated occurrence. We know, looking back, that excessive risk-taking on Wall Street increased in the run-up to the financial crisis. In fact, in my years on Wall Street I saw an almost constant pride in taking risks, and executives firm in their belief that they understood these risks (which, in hindsight, they clearly didn't). It built on itself, and risk increased exponentially as everyone in the industry kept trying to out-risk-take one another.

It's easy to conclude that the cause was overconfidence. But I would argue that this risky behavior was less a cause than a symptom of the crippling groupthink that arose from the lack of diversity on Wall Street—frankly from the lack of women.

It's true, studies show that women are inherently more risk-aware than men. It's why women tend to be better investors than men (that's true for both individual[3] and professional[4] investors). Start-ups with women in their management team have better returns for their investors than male-only ones, and companies with female CFOs are less likely to make value-destroying acquisitions.[5] It's also why women are significantly less likely to speed, to run red lights, and to drive drunk.[6]

I saw this difference in behavior firsthand at Smith Barney. In one case, when we surveyed our clients about one of our products, it was clear that neither men nor women clients understood what that product—a "managed account"—was. Something like 84 percent of them didn't know what it was. Neither the women nor the men were particularly keen to take the time to read the hundreds of pages of disclosure on the product (who could blame them!); nor would either gender really ask their financial advisor what a managed account was. But the difference was that the men would invest in the product despite not knowing what it was, and the women would not. Women didn't understand the risk and so they held back.

So, what can women's risk awareness offer to businesses? For one, a lot more transparency. For another, a lot better decision making. Our risk awareness not only means we make fewer mistakes, it also means we have a greater ability to dial back from mistakes we do make.

What does it look like in action? As leaders and managers, it means recognizing the difference between confidence and competence.[7] It means us actively working to know our blind spots. (Mine is that I am drawn to optimistic people.) It means valuing our intuition when something feels "off." It means embracing this instinct rather than trying to tamp it down, and voicing it rather than staying silent.

It means encouraging an active debate, playing devil's advocate about an idea, to make sure positions have been fully fleshed and thought out. It means discussing what potential downsides to a plan can be, even if "everyone" agrees that the chances of anything going wrong are ridiculously small. It means thanking and celebrating the naysayers and the whistle-blowers, rather than ostracizing and firing them.

It means being willing to voice a different opinion from that of the majority at the table, and listening to the thoughts and opinions of everyone at that table, even—and perhaps especially—those who don't rush to speak. All of this leads to more diversity of thought, which in turn means more creativity and innovation.

When I was running Smith Barney and Merrill Lynch, I made sure that I assessed risk every day. When I was in meetings, I would ask again and again, "What's the 'everybody knows' risk? What's the risk we're not seeing, because we're too close to it?" In other words, what is the thing that everyone has been doing, always—that even the regulators knew about—but that would look bad if we saw it with fresh eyes on the cover of the *Wall Street Journal*?

For me, risk awareness meant working as hard as I could to receive bad news well; that way, no one was ever nervous or scared to bubble business problems up. This went a tremendously long way in keeping little mistakes from becoming big mistakes—and big mistakes from becoming giant mistakes.

I don't think anyone would argue that the world of business is getting any less risky. Indeed, as our world becomes more technology driven, complex, and hyperconnected, it's safe to assume that risk can and will tend to pop up in more and more unexpected places. That means our natural tendency as women to avoid overconfidence and think through risks carefully is only going to become more valuable going forward.

So remember that no matter what your position is in your organization, calling out the risks you see doesn't make you a stick in the mud, or a chicken, or "not a team player." To the contrary, it can often be the most valuable service you can perform for your employer or workplace to say, "Hold on a second. Whoa, Nelly. Let's go over this again."

Trait #2: We Think Big Picture: We're Better at Managing Complexity–and Slower at Ordering in Restaurants

The financial crisis made me reevaluate a lot of what I thought I knew about business. A lot.

One example: if you'd asked me beforehand whether men or women were better at managing complexity—that is, seeing the whole picture before making a business decision—I'd have said men, no question. I would have said they're drawn to it. I would think of my brother in his room when we were kids, building intricate models of ships, hour after hour. And I would think of all those guys I knew growing up tinkering in their garages on old cars, or memorizing obscure baseball statistics.

And I would think of my pre-crisis time on Wall Street, when I saw an industry in which people (mostly men) were constantly building ever-more-complex products. They'd keep adding more and more capabilities, more and more intricate features.

And so I would have said that women were more drawn to simplicity, in business at least. It seemed to me that women were always boiling things down; that's what I saw in the companies I worked for, at least. And that's what I thought I knew.

But now that I've spent time on all this research on gender, I see things differently, and I find myself drawn to an analogy.

We see a man and a woman ordering dinner at a restaurant.

The man barely even looks at the menu. "Steak, medium rare." Meanwhile, the woman is studying the menu like an aspiring lawyer preparing for the bar exam.

"Well," she muses, "a steak would be good. I haven't had a lot of protein lately. But the fish looks fresh and has omega-three and is leaner. Or I could get the salad with chicken, and then I'd still have room for dessert, which would be good because their chocolate mousse is famous. The special looks good, too, but it's expensive, whereas the chicken salad is what they're known for. And garlic prawns sound good, but it's date night so maybe a bunch of garlic isn't the best idea. . . ."

As it happens, this "women linger over menus" thing isn't just a stereotype. Women actually use more parts of their brain when choosing among options. On brain scans, different regions of a woman's brain, across the hemispheres, light up[8] when making a decision, whereas a man's brain activity stays in one region.

As a result, women can be better at evaluating complex situations where men can be frustrated by a wide variety of choices. Put another way, research shows that when complexity rises, men focus on fewer inputs, and thus the quality of their decision making drops, while a woman's remains high.[9] Faced with complicated decisions, rather than trying to render them in black and white, women flourish in analyzing the shades of gray. Thus many studies[10] show that women's brains are better able to manage complexity and to see problems more holistically.

I saw evidence of this during the financial crisis. The men around me, struggling to react to the boatloads of new information streaming at them, kept pulling in the same data in their projections that had worked for them in the past. One mantra I heard, for example, was "Every time the market has done X, it has rebounded by Y."

But of course, this time around, things were different.

This male way of making decisions—decisive, strong—felt

better in the moment. It felt reassuring, as though someone was at the wheel with a firm hand. In our society, value is given to confidence and bold decision making.

In contrast, the deliberating woman at the dinner table, so the thinking in our culture has historically gone, is seen as *in*decisive, and this is thought to make her weak. Not being able to make up your mind quickly is seen in our society as something to overcome. But should it be?

While the waiter may have to circle back to the table once or twice to check on the woman in our story, the way she orders is not inherently flawed. She is juggling the complexity offered by the menu, weighing pros and cons—variables in mood, taste, health, cost—and in doing so she's able to make the best overall choice.

He may be making the quicker and more efficient decision, true; but she is the one likely to end up happier with her meal (and probably with a lower cholesterol count).

This is a trivial yet telling example of the power of holistic thinking in action. It's something women are naturally predisposed to do. And it's not just good for ordering at restaurants; it's very good for business. It can help us see around corners. It can help us identify important patterns; and that means the potential for us to come to smarter, more informed decisions.

I know this ability certainly helped me when my job was investing. As an analyst I had to keep a long list of factors in my head, from interest rates to management initiatives to new products, while also bringing in new data. I wasn't just comfortable juggling all those considerations; I actually enjoyed the process. And this skill—juggling lots of data and details—isn't useful only in investing; it's invaluable in just about any job I can think of.

And it's a skill that's becoming all the more valuable, as the world is only becoming more information-rich.

We can see this in something as everyday as our morning

routines. When I started as a research analyst, I consumed my news—in the form of the *Wall Street Journal* and the *New York Times* business section—on the subway on the way to work. In hindsight, it feels like a pretty relaxed start to the day.

Today, I pick up my phone when the alarm goes off and I'm consuming news from hundreds of sources all over the world, before I even brush my teeth. And I continue to read and listen all day long and into the night. Sure, some amount of it is cat videos; but those aside, I, like most people, take in significantly more information compared to not so many years ago.

On a larger scale, the business world is becoming more complex as it becomes inexorably more global and more hyperconnected. No matter what business we are in, today the vast majority of us are interacting with colleagues, customers, and clients from other cultures; experiencing different value systems; and navigating a wider swath of rules, norms, and perspectives than ever before.

The barrage of information and the rise in connectivity that we are experiencing today make the ability to see patterns among data ever more important. We have more information than ever to filter and process, and more choices to make about how to weigh it, and then factor it into our decisions.

When we're managing this complexity well, we spend time on the "what-ifs." And then we spend even more time on more "what-ifs." This in turn predisposes us to evaluate choices from all angles, conduct postmortems of projects, and learn from what unexpected factors popped up, and where the surprises were.

For me, both as a research analyst and a newly minted entrepreneur, my initial approach to managing complexity was perhaps counterintuitive. I would slosh around in the information for a while, then I would dive into the details, learning as much as I could. And I would work to hold back judgment on what details mattered and what didn't; instead I would just soak it all in.

Doing this would often allow patterns and relationships to emerge over time. I can't tell you how often my unconscious would go to work on a complicated issue and then seemingly out of the blue present me with an insight, popping into my head first thing in the morning or after a glass of wine at night. (For example, for years, it was not at all unusual for me to wake up in the morning just knowing I had made a mistake in one of my Excel spreadsheets . . . and what the mistake was. And when I fired up my computer, that mistake was always sitting there, waiting for me.)

Problem solving is one of the most essential abilities in just about any job and in just about every aspect of life. It doesn't matter if the problem you're solving is which new client or project to go after, how best to solve a UX puzzle, or what to order at a restaurant: the ability to manage complexity by seeing the whole picture is critical to making a successful decision.

Often this ability must be augmented by bringing diversity of thought to the problem; thus many of today's stickiest problems—in business and elsewhere—require more than one brain to solve. Fortunately, as we'll see in the next section, we women are also good at building the kinds of relationships and connections—with our colleagues, our customers, our clients— that help us not only in managing complexity, but also in other ways that can elevate our careers, our reputations, and more.

Trait #3: We're Relationship-Focused: How Making Connections Helps Us, Our Companies, and the Bottom Line

You probably have plenty of anecdotal evidence to back up the idea that women are particularly strong at registering other people's emotions. And for some guys it's not their . . . well . . . strong suit. I still laugh when I remember one of my senior male colleagues repeatedly assuring his boss that one of his employees would be "completely fine" with some management changes being made—right before that employee stormed out, turned off his cellphone for the day, and refused to come back to the office—ever. (Yes, this really happened.)

But anecdotal evidence aside, there is research to back up the claim that women are more empathetic, better connectors, and natural relationship-builders—all skills that matter enormously for success in business. For one thing, women outperform men on emotional intelligence (so-called EQ), which is all about reading people and forging relationships.[11] And in terms of the *types* of relationships the genders prefer, another study found that men prefer large, all-male groups, while women nurture intimate friendships.[12] As a result, we women in the workplace tend to bond more—with customers, with the receptionist, with the interns, with the mailman, with the boss—which not only makes us great collaborators and valuable team players, but also gives us a greater sense of purpose at work.

And with this relationship focus comes a major opportunity for us women as the pace of technological change continues to accelerate and more jobs are threatened by machine learning and automation. Why? Think about the types of jobs that no robot or algorithm could ever replace. Manager. Psychologist or social worker. Doctor or nurse. Drug counselor. Consultant. Elementary school teacher. What do these jobs have in common? They all rely on intrinsically human traits—such as relationship-building, empathy, and compassion.

What are the benefits for our companies as a result of our relationship focus? Well, one is greater engagement; as a Gallup poll[13] found, employees of female managers were on average six percentage points more engaged than those working for a male manager; and, in fact, employees of female managers outscored male managers on eleven out of twelve measures of engagement. And this is great, because in turn high employee engagement improves every business performance number: profitability, productivity, quality, and customer loyalty.[14]

The first time I really thought about the effects of relationship focus on business was when I visited a head of investor relations at a company I covered as a research analyst. He kept a photo of the top shareholder of his company across from his desk on his bulletin board. A guy who hadn't bought the stock yesterday, but who had owned it for years and years. And who would likely own it for years and years more. I asked him why he had that photo and he said, "I need to remember these aren't faceless names. I need to remember that these are real people. I am working for this guy."

There is no question that customer focus is something that women bring to work—in spades. And this is a big deal because doing the right thing for the customer is so essential to success in any business. But it's not always that easy, as I learned during my time on Wall Street.

Let's head back to Sanford Bernstein, the place where I had made the controversial, risk-aware—but right—stock call on American General. After some time covering the life insurance industry, I graduated to covering the more high-profile industry of Wall Street itself, found success there, and was subsequently offered the job of director of research. (I recall noting at the time that I would be managing a group of analysts who were pretty much all older than me and a lot more male—something that would become a bit of a theme for me over the years.)

I received that promotion in 1999 and was only the fifth person to hold the position at the company. Coming into the challenging role—my first management one—I tried to examine the new job as a research analyst would a company, assessing the opportunities, considering the risks, and in general trying to look around corners. I tried to think about the business not as one that sold financial services, but rather as one that served *people.*

At the time, most research departments on Wall Street had two sets of clients that they advised ... two sets of clients whose interests were, by definition, in conflict. One set was the investing clients—they wanted to use our research to find stocks to buy on the cheap (and sell when they were expensive). The other set of clients was the corporate ones—they wanted to issue stock in their companies at a high price. One group, in other words, wanted to "buy low." The other wanted to "sell high."

For someone in my position these different interests presented a conundrum: do right by one group, and you could do wrong by the other.

As I thought through this, it seemed to me that this fundamental conflict of interest represented a real business risk for us (yes, there's that word again). If we wanted to be truly client focused (in this case on the investing clients), how could we also work seemingly against their interests?

The solution, as I saw it, was to withdraw from the investment banking business so we could focus on serving—truly serving—our investing clients. When I took this to the CEO of Bernstein, the arguments against our withdrawing from the investment banking business were many. First up, it would cost us millions of dollars in revenue. (And we didn't make billions of dollars, as some of the other firms did, so forgoing millions of dollars really meant something for the business.) Second, it could hurt our employees—the research analysts—because that lost revenue stream potentially meant we would pay them less than our competitors could. Heck, even our investing clients—for whom we were doing it—told us it was a bad idea; I remember one telling me he thought we should stay in the investment banking game, since more revenue would allow us to invest more in our business, accruing eventually to his benefit as a client. Final argument for not exiting the underwriting business: no one else was. Not a single one of our competitors. It was a seemingly crazy idea that no one else had tried. (I'll never forget the then director of research at Goldman Sachs helpfully mansplaining this for me—before mansplaining was a thing.)

We did it anyway. We got out of the business; we gave up the revenue. It just seemed like the only way to do right by the investing clients—the people—we served.

And . . . this was a losing business strategy for years. We lost analysts to other firms that paid more; we gained the reputation among the other firms as being stodgy and out of it; we seemed hopelessly second tier. Let's just say that a job at Bernstein in those days wasn't much to brag about at a cocktail party. The word was that maybe you started your career at Bernstein, but you got out of there to go work at a "big boy" firm at some point.

And then . . . the Internet bubble[15] of the late 1990s burst. Investors lost money, lots of money. And where money is lost, there are always lawyers. And New York attorney general Eliot Spitzer began to investigate. His findings: that some of our competitors were plagued by that same conflict of interest we had gotten out of investment banking to avoid; that is, analysts were telling investors to buy a stock in public, but in private emails they referred to them as "POSes," or pieces of—well, you know. And this type of behavior wasn't happening at just one firm; it was going on at several, including some of the storied names.

So it turned out that those millions of dollars in revenues that we at Bernstein gave up were more than regained by not having to pay the *hundreds* of millions of dollars in regulatory fines that our competitors did. Not to mention, of course, the cost in reputation, which could not be calculated.

That was how, in the spring of 2002, I found myself on the cover of *Fortune* magazine, with a pretty much life-size, close-up picture of my face and the headline "The Last Honest Analyst."

I know, wow, right? The bet on client focus—and relationship focus—paid off.

At Ellevest, too, we work to be client-focused at our core, engaging with the women in our market all of the time. We're constantly user testing, user testing, and user testing to the point that I would say we are "co-creating" the business with our clients. We spent significant time with "Elle" before we wrote the first line of code; we're engaging with her in person and online because we believe it's important for us to "meet her where she is," to work closely with her to see what resonates and what doesn't in our offering. It's not about what I think the right approach is for Ellevest; she's helping us find it. She is shaping the product to a degree that was simply never thought of at my previous big-company job.

In my career I found that my way of managing—my very *female* way of managing—was all about listening, really listening, to those on my team, as well as to our customers. I didn't pretend I was listening, believing I had "the answer" the whole time.

Whether we manage one person or one hundred, owning our relationship focus makes us better leaders. The days of the boss as "hard-ass" need to be kissed good-bye. Today the business world increasingly values the kind of leaders who recognize that their employees' lives don't begin and end when they are at work. Many of us have families, and pets, and outside interests, and medical needs, and hobbies. Really, it's well past time to get over requiring face time. And work as an extreme sport, complete with all-nighters and last-minute business trips—it isn't good for employees, and it certainly doesn't allow anyone to do their best work; and younger professionals are turning away from it in droves. Why not own the fact that we are all people and acknowledge that all of us need time for our outside lives?

It's just smart business.

Trait #4: We Think Long-Term: How Women Combat Dangerous Shortsightedness

When I speak to women entrepreneurs today about why they started their businesses, the first answer is typically "to build the type of business at which I want to work." I also hear that they started their businesses because they wanted to bring to the world a product or service that was missing. And right on the heels of those answers is the desire to build a business for the long term.

When you raise money for a business, a great many investors will ask you about your "exit strategy"—that is, whether you plan to sell the company or take it public. "Exit strategy?" so many women I know say. "I don't have an exit strategy. I want to build this for years."

You know that I'm about to contrast this attitude to Wall Street's, right?

When I was there, the mantra was always "This quarter is the most important quarter ever." That meant our goal was to "make the numbers," that is, to deliver the highest possible quarterly earnings to our shareholders ... every three months ... which meant that the bosses often made decisions that were good in the short term but disastrous in the long.

I saw this starkly when I was the chief financial officer of Citigroup. I had one particularly memorable encounter with a group of buy-side investors who had come to visit for a business update. Now, the people who came by that day were not high-frequency traders or hedge fund managers looking to make a quick buck. These were, in theory, plain-vanilla, salt-of-the-earth mutual fund managers, the kind of people you hire to help you invest your retirement savings.

When one of them, a portfolio manager at a brand-name asset management firm, asked our CEO, "What are your growth projections for Citigroup?" our fearless leader gave a very ambitious prediction—one that had the bank growing at a rate quite a bit faster than the global economy would grow. *Hmm*, you might say. *But no huge bank can grow at multiples of economic growth for any reasonable period of time, can it?* And you would be right; it can't. Or it can't safely.

Yet despite this overly optimistic projection, this Little Lord Fauntleroy of a portfolio manager was unimpressed. He very obviously rolled his eyes and let out a big, dramatic sigh. (They say that an eye roll signifies barely disguised contempt. Well, this contempt was not disguised at all.)

I had a couple of thoughts in that moment, one of which was, *You jerk. What would your parents think of you rolling your eyes like that in a business meeting?* The other: *Uh-oh.*

As soon as the meeting was over, the CEO pulled me aside and said, "We need to leverage the company up." What he meant was, we needed to take on more financial risk to grow more quickly, and we needed to do it now. (While other ways of driving growth, like opening up new branches, can take years to pay off, taking on more leverage can generate results fast.)

Time and time again, I saw this conflict between "deliver now" and "deliver over time." And time and time again I saw how the de facto decision to deliver now hurt both the company and its customers and clients. And this isn't common only on Wall Street; many leaders in business today can look for shortcuts to drive stocks higher in the near term instead of taking a long-term view of what can drive sustainable growth in a company.

And this takes a heavy toll. The 2010 Aspen Institute report[16] showed that when companies want to be more profitable in the near term, they will put off investing in research and development, which means less innovation, less invention, and fewer breakthroughs in the long run.[17]

So, how do you combat short-termism?

One answer: women. (You knew I was going to say that.)

Research shows that women—and this goes hand in hand with our natural tendency to think through risk—are good at looking to the long term. That long-term focus can be extremely valuable to our employers, and in turn it can help us.

Long-term thinking isn't just about thinking about what effect decisions will have next week or next month. It's about looking at what they will mean in a year, five years, twenty years. In our careers this might mean that we take a job that pays a lower salary or make a lateral move in order to be on the ladder we want to climb.

This long-term thinking about our career trajectory is especially important for women. Men tend to work straight through their careers and peak at a somewhat earlier age, while women take more breaks and then can work longer, because they live longer. (Don't believe me? Four words: Bill and Hillary Clinton. I think we can all agree that one's career peaks when one is president of the United States . . . so clearly he peaked earlier than she did.)

So we women should strive to work at companies that allow those natural career rhythms to occur and won't penalize us for career breaks. This means we need to recognize that an employee's contribution should be measured over years, not months. We need more companies that support the taking of sabbaticals and offer generous flex policies so people can take breaks and tend to their private lives, making them more productive and loyal in the long term.

For an entrepreneur, long-term thinking can mean spending more time on creating a business plan to ensure you get it right, or investing more effort in building your product so it will last. It can mean putting off going public, in part to avoid the quarterly earnings pressure of markets. And it can mean choosing investors who will be long-term partners; at Ellevest, for example, we didn't just look for those investors to fund the start-up of the business who would give us the best terms; instead we worked to find investors who were proven to take a long-term approach to building businesses.

From what I've seen in my career, many people are too focused on short-term wins, whether in the stock market or in their careers or even in their personal lives. Society has conditioned us to always be on the lookout for shortcuts, to look at life as one big race to the finish line. But as the old fable of the tortoise and the hare taught us, it's the slow and steady approach that wins the race most of the time.

Trait #5: We Love to Learn: How Women Keep Companies Ahead of the Curve

I loved running Smith Barney.

I only liked running Merrill Lynch.

And a few years ago, I had the opportunity to take a job similar to them both. One late spring morning, I was walking up Madison Avenue in Manhattan, on the way to agree to the final details of that job, feeling pretty good about things, when . . . *WHAM!*

I'm not sure exactly how it happened, but I fell, and I fell hard. And I fell fast. So fast, in fact, that I didn't manage to get my hands out to catch myself. Instead I went down, chin-first, onto a subway grate. It still gives me the chills to remember how sudden and unexpected it felt. And how painful it was.

My purse went flying, my bracelet broke and went flying, and my shoes came off. As they say in skiing, it was a "yard sale."

I jumped up, and my first thought was, *I can still make it to my meeting.*

Then I spit out a tooth, noticed my blood dripping onto the sidewalk, and thought better of it.

The inventory: one broken tooth, four stitches in my chin, a dislocated jaw, a hairline fracture in my jaw, bleeding knees, whiplash, and double vision. And of course, that broken bracelet. And my pride.

I've never been one to believe in signs from above, but if there is such a thing as a sign not to take a job, I'm pretty sure that was it. So I slowed that job process down and, as I drank my meals through a straw for the next month, I tried to be introspective about why I had *loved* my time at Smith Barney but only *liked* my time at Merrill Lynch.

At both I enjoyed working with my teams, as well as with financial advisors whom I genuinely admired and liked. Both businesses had important missions of helping families plan for their futures. Both were in need of turnarounds when I arrived, so both jobs were deeply engaging and challenging.

The difference, I concluded over many hours of pain pills and liquid kale, was that at the first one I was *learning and doing.* Given the similarities of the two, the second was much more doing, and less learning. But I, like so many professional women I know, love to learn.

I loved school. I loved shopping for school supplies. I loved the smell of a brand-new pencil case and the feel of a crisp new notebook with my name written inside. In college I loved cracking the books on the first day. I loved signing up for classes outside my major. I loved signing up for classes in my major. I loved getting A's. Really loved getting A's. Heck, I even loved exams.

(I recently got a text from my daughter, who's studying at my alma mater, the University of North Carolina at Chapel Hill, asking me if it's crazy that she really likes exams. It warmed my heart.)

And it's not just me. Increasingly, I've recognized that we women love to learn and that we do better at jobs at which we're acquiring new skills. Indeed, we are educated as never before. We're 57 percent of college graduates and 62 percent of master's degree grads.[18] And we don't just love to learn; we're also good at it: a recent analysis found girls making higher grades than boys overall.[19] (Of course, these two qualities are related: think about how many females you know who love turning over that graded test and seeing that shiny A.)

This learning orientation extends into the workplace, with so many women defining career success partly by whether they continue to learn and challenge themselves. In fact, 89 percent of Ellevate Network members say that the opportunity to learn is very important in accepting a new job, and another 10 percent say it's a consideration.[20] That's a total of 99 percent who value learning; it doesn't get much higher than that!

This love of learning is more valuable than ever now that the pace of change in business is speeding up.[21] Think about it: it took the better part of a century for telephones to become ubiquitous, but smartphones have been around only since about 2002, and look at how omnipresent they are today. It took thirty years for electricity to reach a 10 percent adoption rate; it took tablet devices less than five years to get to that point. Even five years ago, the design cycle for cars was 60 months; now it's 24–36 months. The Internet has been around only since about 1990 and is now in more than 60 percent of homes, whereas it took dishwashers more than fifty years to get to the same level of adoption. The message is clear: things are moving much, much faster. Which means there is that much more to learn.

Not surprisingly, then, in a recent survey of professionals by Accenture, 91 percent said that the most successful employees are those able to adapt to a changing workplace.[22]

And going forward, as the pace of change continues to accelerate, learning will become even that much more important, particularly when it comes to advancing our careers.

You don't need me to tell you that this all means that career trajectories are changing, too. The old way: starting at one company in the training program, doing the same type of work for forty years at increasingly senior levels (while doing less and less of the actual work, and taking longer and longer weekends), and retiring from that same company with a gold watch.

But in our times of constant change, this old way is out with yesterday's recycling. Today people work at a company for 4.4 years on average. Indeed, the data shows that "job-hopping" is increasing. Millennials could have fifteen to twenty jobs in the course of their lives.[23]

So what does adjusting to this new way require? You guessed it: constant learning. In this kind of environment, the mindset of life-long learning will be an increasingly valuable attribute, because this is the mindset that enables us to adapt to change.

Today it's not enough to land the job and learn as we go. We need to learn the skills for a job, get the job, then learn *new* skills required to stay competitive and relevant as the demands of that job—and the technology needed to meet them—evolve. And not just as newbies starting out; this process will likely repeat itself not once but several times throughout our careers.

I've seen this stark shift in my own life. My father is a lawyer in his seventies, and he was a lawyer in his twenties, his thirties, his forties, his fifties, and his sixties. I was an (unhappy and not particularly good) investment banker in my twenties, a research analyst in my thirties, a manager of complex wealth management businesses in my forties, and am now an entrepreneur in my fifties. These shifts were driven as much by my drive to keep learning and changing as by how the business world has been changing.

With these changes come opportunities; ones that weren't available a handful of years ago are available now. Today we all have the ability to reinvent ourselves several times over the course of our careers (more on this in chapter 8). We have the ability to leave companies, start companies, even invent new kinds of companies. Today we can do almost anything, as long as we are committed to learning.

I see any number of women capitalizing on these changes. How?

Well, first I see many women going back to school for that extra degree or taking classes at night or on weekends to work on new skills. I'm hearing more and more women talking about their "side hustle," that is, a part-time job separate from their full-time job; for many, it can be not just a way of earning extra income but also a means of learning and expanding their skill set and earning more.

We're also reaching out more for mentoring, and getting better at keeping up on the latest trends in businesses.

We're joining advisory or nonprofit boards to expand our knowledge and our networks.

We're educating ourselves because we love it—and because we recognize how important it is for the long-term success of our careers.

Smart companies that recognize the importance of continuous learning are committing themselves to educating their workforce on the latest skills and technology in order to keep their people engaged and their skill sets valuable. This can include offering career sabbaticals so that employees can explore outside interests, gain new skills and knowledge, and bring that new expertise back to the workplace. Talk about a win-win. While it takes an investment on the part of companies, it's one that can pay off for the business and the individual in ways that positively impact both morale and productivity—and thus the bottom line.

And these types of opportunities are becoming more accessible, thanks, of course, to the Internet. For example, sites like Skillcrush and Skillshare teach online classes in coding and programming. Lynda.com provides online tutorials on Web design and app development, design and photography, marketing and sales, and more, and online universities like Khan Academy and Udemy provide an absolute wealth of classes on topics from organic chemistry to world history to mechanical engineering, and it's all either free or far less expensive than traditional classroom learning.

So opportunities to learn are rising as the need and desire to continue to learn increase. And more and more of us women are taking advantage of them—as we should be—as a means to becoming more indispensable to our companies and invest in owning our futures.

Trait #6: We Care About the *Why:* Money Is Important—But So Are Meaning and Purpose . . . and, Newsflash (!), They Aren't Mutually Exclusive

I've saved my favorite quality for last: our desire for meaning and purpose in all aspects of our lives. This is a great, great attribute (I mean, who wouldn't want to have meaning and purpose, right?) and has the potential to have an outsize impact on business and our society—not to mention our own careers.

Now, I fully recognize that this can only be a top priority for us when we are solid in our jobs or career paths. If we are just starting out, or if we are insecure in our positions, finding meaning and purpose in our work might have to take a backseat to other, more practical concerns (like a steady paycheck, or getting a foothold in the industry where we want to build our careers). But for many women, as we build professional stability, the desire to have an impact on the world around us—particularly through our work, where we all spend so much of our time—moves to the forefront.

I, for one, am completely solid in my professional mission to help women reach their professional and financial goals and close their own gender money gaps. But this mission is one I've discovered only in the past few years. That's why I'm writing this book now, and why I decided to throw myself face-first, with Ellevest, into the risky and often terrifying life of an entrepreneur.

But I deeply believe it's worth it. Why? Well, first off, remember that women exercise decision-making control on roughly $11.2 trillion of investable assets in the United States.[24] Yet we women don't invest our money to the same degree that men do. By some estimates, the majority of our money is in the bank, not working harder for us in the stock and bond markets. And that's in large part because women don't feel served by existing financial services. In one report roughly three-quarters of women said they were "most dissatisfied" with the existing industry on a service and product level.[25]

So filling that gap—providing women with investment strategies and services tailored to their needs—really felt like something I was called to help do, given my background and given the importance of the issue. I have become convinced that revolutionizing the financial services system for women is a mission I want to pursue.

I'm not unique in being motivated by a professional mission. Not by a long shot. Through the Ellevate Network, I've seen so many women looking to make a mark that goes beyond "making a living." In fact, in surveys they say that the number one thing they look for in their work is "meaning and purpose." In contrast, when men take those same surveys, the number one reason they give for accepting a job is money.[26] For professional women, money comes fourth, after the opportunity to learn and working with a great team. Further, in our polling of Ellevate, we found that 57 percent of women say that they have a "professional mission"; another 16 percent said they were working on it.[27]

In short, finding purpose in one's work and one's life matters to a great many women. This may mean working at a company that has an explicit social mission, or it may mean finding value in one's existing job or role. I will never forget those days at Bernstein following the attacks of September 11, 2001; most of us were in no mood to drag ourselves back to work. In good times the equity research business could feel almost like a game: Could your stock picks outperform the market? Could you publish a piece of research that piqued clients' interest? Could you be the first to spot that hot new stock or investment—before the rest of the market caught wind? But who really cared about those sorts of things after 9/11, when we had lost so many friends and former colleagues?

But at the time, Bernstein's then–associate director of research, the amazing Lisa Shalett, reminded us that we had an even more important job. I remember her noting that the market would be enormously volatile in the aftermath of the attack, and so the reasoned guidance we could provide our clients would have more value than ever. In other words, the craft of equity research no longer felt like a game; it felt essential. I felt like our work was important, and let me tell you, that feeling made me want to get back to work in a way that the promise of a year-end bonus never could.

Studies show that there can be an actual financial boon to companies that provide their employees with meaning and a sense of purpose in their work. It's not rocket science: if we believe in what our companies are doing, and if we are committed to our companies on a deep level, we will have better morale, which means we will be more motivated to work harder, which also means we will be more likely to deliver better results. Moreover, starting a business that has a positive effect on the world has never been easier. Thanks to the plummeting cost of technology and the explosion of services to support new businesses, more and more women— and men—are starting mission-driven businesses . . . and reaping substantial profits in the process.

Just look at start-ups like Warby Parker, Tom's, Honest Company, and Stella & Dot, which put purpose front and center in who they are. At Warby Parker and Tom's, for every one of their products you buy (glasses or shoes, respectively), they give one to an individual who can't afford them. Stella & Dot's mission is all about offering flexible entrepreneurship opportunities that promote the economic inclusion of women; they are as much about providing individuals with a means to make a living as they are about selling beautiful jewelry. At Jessica Alba's Honest Company, values are also the driving force of the business; yes, it's cosmetics and baby stuff, but it's also about funding research and education and creating products that are good both for us and for the environment.

What I see every day in my work with Ellevate Network is that more and more successful companies are putting meaning and purpose front and center. They are talking about values and purpose in town halls, and really listening to what their employees have to say about the issues they care about. And they are putting their money where their proverbial mouths are: I recently encountered one company that gives every employee a day off a month so they can volunteer for a cause of their choice—whether at their kid's school or at Habitat for Humanity or at a soup kitchen.

What I see in workplaces like those are people who believe in what they do and who, as a result, are not only happier but also more effective. Employees who feel that their work is important don't watch the clock crawl toward 5 p.m., or get a stomachache on Sunday night, or phone it in at a job that feels disconnected to who they are in their "real" lives.

Think about it this way: A woman who is being paid fairly and treated well can bring a lot to the workplace. But a woman who has those things *and* a sense that her work is valuable—and making a difference in the world ? She's unstoppable.

PART II

Put Your Oxygen Mask On First Before Assisting Others

What is it that they say on airplanes? Put your oxygen mask on first before assisting others.

It always struck me as odd. Really? I'm going to be putting on my oxygen mask while my precious, adorable, love-of-my-life child is gasping for air beside me? But, of course, if I suffocate to death, I'm not there to take care of her, which is bad for her (and not particularly good for me, either).

The point is that if we as women want to capitalize on and accelerate the positive changes in the business world and make that world better for our children, we need to get our oxygen masks on first. We need to position ourselves well for the coming changes in the workplace.

Before you sigh and roll your eyes at all the work you may think you're going to need to do to get there, or all the changes in yourself you might think you need to make, let me start by telling you: You're doing the vast majority of the hard work already! You're already going to work every day, you're already delivering the project on time, you're already landing the new client, you're already making sure the i's are dotted and the t's are crossed.

So not a lot of extra effort can yield a lot of return. That's because what we're going to talk about in this section of the book won't mean changing ourselves, but instead investing in the unique traits and strengths that we as women bring to the table, making us invaluable to our companies, and putting ourselves in the best possible position to lead and succeed at work.

There will be a good return on that effort for your career. But I'm also talking about "return" in a very literal and concrete way. The money way. As in we will talk about how you can capitalize on your natural strengths in ways that will allow you to earn more over the course of your career (yes, by asking for the raise, but even more than that—by learning how to negotiate to increase your value as a professional and how to position yourself for the raise). I'm also going to give you the best career advice that no one is talking about: how to achieve the kind of financial security that will allow you to take more risks (the smart kind) to advance your career.

I don't mean to get all late-night-TV-infomercial on you, but the combination of these has the potential to not just put you in better financial shape, but in much, much better financial shape. Life-changing financial shape.

Let's get started.

CHAPTER 3

Make Sure Success Is Well Defined

So now we're about to get into the good stuff: what we as women can do to own all these amazing attributes to get ahead in our careers. But before we can tap into our growing power for greater career success and all the good stuff that comes with it, we need to get clear on one thing: what that success looks like—for us. And to our bosses. It seems obvious, but you'd be surprised by how many of us never stop to ask that question. And this is a shame, because as I've seen time and time again, knowing what we're working toward can make or break our careers.

Let's start with the "make."

Now, I know it can be a tough sell to recommend Wall Street as a career choice for new graduates these days. But there's one job there that I *would* recommend to younger professionals, and perhaps particularly to women. It's sell-side equity research (that is, analyzing companies and making research-based predictions on future earnings for the purpose of advising clients on how to invest). Seriously! It was the job that I started in my late twenties, and I can honestly say it was the first job I truly loved.

Here's why: To be a successful research analyst, you have to analyze, write, present, and interact with really smart people. So the skill set is varied. The end goal is to make a recommendation to investors to buy or sell a stock. So you have to make and defend your advice. You have to make decisions—lots of them—based on imperfect information. Stocks trade five days a week, so in theory your latest recommendation on a stock is broadcast every minute that the stock trades. This makes it exciting and fast paced.

By no means do you ever have all the information needed to make that stock recommendation. But you *do* have (mostly) the same information as your competitors, and your job is to pull together that information in a coherent way. Then, based on that, you have to determine if the stock of the company you are covering is a buy or a sell.

Pertinent information can change, sometimes often (just because a stock was a "sell" yesterday doesn't mean that it is today). And so you have to keep incorporating new information rapidly (we're pretty good at that, remember?). If you're going to be successful, you learn to do this quickly and analytically.

And you do all of this in public. There is nowhere to hide, so all those lessons are learned the hard way. Since there always seems to be any number of people who love to point out mistakes, you get lots of "help" on this.

To be successful, you have to get comfortable with sometimes having a different view than the consensus of your usually pretty-smart competitors. It's the nonconsensus calls that can be the great ones.

You analyze the information, draw a conclusion, and then you're right or wrong. In other words, success is clear. Failure is clear. Crystal clear. You know exactly what is expected of you—exactly what constitutes success—and you get a real-time reading on whether you've met those expectations. So success is well defined.

Well, okay, maybe it doesn't sound like your cup of tea, but I loved it. I loved every minute of it. I knew what it took to be successful in that job, and I worked hard at it.

But you don't have to be a research analyst to define success for yourself in such clear terms. Today, thanks in part to the massive shifts in business we talked about in earlier chapters, we can all more clearly define what success looks like in our job or position.

Why is it so important, in particular for us women? You know those gender biases that are unfortunately still all too present in most workplaces? When the metrics for success are clear, a lot of that falls away. After all, when the stock a female analyst recommends takes off, while the stock her male colleague is recommending crashes, it's hard to argue that the man is performing better, isn't it? And this is true not just in investing, but in any situation where there are clear metrics and quantifiable results.

Here's a telling example: When I was running Merrill Lynch in the wake of the downturn, we needed to restructure the company's "field organization." There were simply too many people in mid-level management, in too many layers. At the time of the restructuring, we were transitioning to a more metrics-based approach of evaluating our management team, but it wasn't yet fully "burnt in."

The gentleman who was charged with this project came to me with his recommendation for staffing changes.

"I recommend Jonathan for the Midwest job," he told me. "Jonathan took his branches, which started off in terrible shape, and turned them around. He's been with Merrill for a long time and has excelled in every job he has taken on.

"I recommend Steve for the Northeast job," he continued. "Steve is one of our top performers and is particularly strong in transitioning the business from a transactional one to one that is more fee based.

"I recommend Stan for the southern region. Stan has a tough group of employees but leads the country in . . ."

You get the point. Jonathan, Steve, and Stan. And Bob and Jim and Stu. Just one woman, and by the way, none of them was a person of color.

At one point he said to me, "I wish I could recommend more diverse individuals for these jobs. But the results are the results, and *we want to put the best person in each job*."

My response was that he certainly seemed to have been thoughtful on his choices. But . . . before we made the final decisions, could he please pull together the new manager scorecards that we'd developed? So could I see the business results that backed up his recommendations?

He came back to my office two days later with his proverbial tail between his legs. Some of the people he had recommended had indeed generated the best business results, but some had not. They had simply done the best job of "spinning" their results or of communicating their wins to him. He had fallen under the spell of overconfidence.

Once the numbers were placed side by side, however, the lens shifted. The winners and losers were clear, and as a result more women and diverse individuals ended up in the prime seats.

So, making sure success is well defined mattered here.

But it's more than simply about putting the best performers in the right jobs. Because when success is quantifiable, you don't have to worry about superficial nonsense like "face time," or staying at your desk until 9 p.m. twiddling your thumbs to prove to your boss just how "dedicated" you are; I always like to say that I never had a research report rejected by a client because I had written it on a Sunday evening, after the kids were asleep, rather than a Thursday afternoon in the office. Even though I worked enormously hard, having success well defined gave me some great job flexibility, at a time in my life when I needed it most.

And of course, these advantages hold true for any job in which success and failure are well defined, not just on Wall Street.

Failing to get clarity on what success looks like is a common mistake, and one that I've made myself. For example, I didn't ask about the metrics for success when I got "the call" back in August 2009 to run Merrill Lynch, and I paid for that oversight. Dearly.

It seemed like a dream come true. Bank of America had bought Merrill in the beginning of 2009 when Merrill was going under in the financial crisis. But the early days of the acquisition did not go well, and by that summer, Merrill was hemorrhaging financial advisors at an historic rate. As a result, they were looking to make a management change. As I understand it, Ken Lewis, then-CEO of Bank of America, called my old boss, Sandy Weill, and got the thumbs-up that I had the skills needed to put together the leadership team and the strategy to turn around the business.

Boy, did I want that job. I had been booted out of Smith Barney by the new Citi CEO, and so the opportunity to get back into the business—heck, to run a business that was larger than my old one—and to have the opportunity to turn it around . . . well, it felt too good to be true.

You know what they say about things that seem too good to be true? They usually are.

So I ignored every warning sign. I ignored it when the folks at Bank of America wouldn't let me meet my soon-to-be colleagues; I ignored it when they wouldn't allow me to meet any members of the board; I ignored it when they told me that there could be no compensation guarantee because, they said, the regulators wouldn't allow it. Most important, I ignored the fact that they didn't give me a clear picture of what was expected of me and what success in this job would look like. We would come to that agreement together, later.

Before I joined, the CEO said he wanted to be straight with me. The financial crisis had exhausted him; he was thinking about retiring. But . . . he would stay at Bank of America for two more years, which would give me time to steady my sea legs. He would coach me; he had my back. And I had his word.

Well, he didn't wait two years to announce his retirement. He announced it less than two *months* later.

Cue the music from *Jaws*, because this is the moment when the warning voice that lives in the pit of my stomach told me I should never have taken this job. And, indeed, when the successor as CEO told me what my compensation would be that year, it turned out to be notably less than the number I'd been cited as part of the handshake agreement I'd had with the old CEO. Worse, I quickly learned that the ongoing performance assessment at the company was some convoluted combination of how the business did versus budget (which meant *a lot* of time negotiating to get lower budgets approved), relative performance rankings within departments, and anonymous 360-degree reviews.

In other words, the bar for success was not clear. Other people navigated it well and some tried to help me: I'll never forget one of my colleagues taking me aside to tell me the ins and outs of "how the game was played." (Not exactly the "meaning and purpose" I was looking for in my career.)

The worst thing about incentive plans like this is that they can pit employees against one another for the same scarce bonus dollars. What happens when you can potentially get more of that money by tearing others down via anonymous reviews? The knives can come out. And then so do the tissues.

When performance is based on subjective metrics like how you're doing in relation to the guy at the desk next to you, there can be little clarity around what success is or isn't. Instead it can be based on things that can feel beyond one's control. Even worse, this can set up a situation in which the inherent gender biases that we all know exist can be unchecked. (An anonymous 360-degree review? An absolute breeding ground for it. I remember one of mine, where I was called out for being too direct *and* too indirect in my leadership communications, a well-known "double bind" for women.)

So I would argue that the first thing to think about when weighing whether to take a position is this: is the definition of success clear? Second, and also important is, how will you be compensated for that success? I've spoken with any number of people about this over the years, and am always amazed by how rarely those questions get asked.

If you only take one thing away from this chapter, it's that having agreed-upon goals and metrics with your boss—and, even better, having agreement on how you'll be compensated if you meet those goals, if you're able—is a means to putting you in control of your business life. Sure, that means there is a risk that you will miss them, but how can you have any hope of meeting or exceeding your goals if you don't even know what they are?

So no matter what industry or field you work in, or what stage you are at in your career, at every turn it's worth asking: What does success mean here? And what does it take for people to see me as successful? Are those two things the same? Do they make sense? Are they within reach?

Every time you take a new job or promotion, please sit down with your boss and find out what the expectations are. And in turn be honest about what you feel you will be able to promise. It's much easier to set expectations at the very beginning than to try to roll them back later. Believe me, I've seen that movie too many times, and it doesn't end well. Getting a plan in place up front wins, hands down, every time.

Moreover, if you don't agree with the company's measure of success—for example, if a company only values delivering "the numbers" for shareholders and does not measure and value customer satisfaction—that conversation can alert you to red flags that this may not be the right job or company for you. Conversely, if you feel like the goals being set for you are aligned with yours, if they're exciting and give you a sense of purpose, that can be a wonderful position to be in.

A final note: so many jobs these days (and even more going forward) require collaboration. Recall that this is something we women are awfully good at, because of our relationship focus.

But there's a big "but." We women have been less likely to get credit for collaborating than the guys do; this means that when our success is measured by our team's rather than our individual performance, we can end up with the short end of the stick.[1]

One solution is to make sure that you own discrete parts of a project and can point to what you contributed. Another is to take on a role as project spokesperson; if you are in front of the room talking about a project and taking ownership of it, you will become associated with its success. A third approach is to make sure that you take credit for your portion of the work; work it into conversations, talk about what it did for the bottom line, talk about how it helps customers, talk about how it furthered the company's strategy or reputation, talk about the learnings from it. Own it.

If you're thinking, *I don't want to brag,* then don't. Don't brag. But do work your achievements into the conversation, in an objective, quantifiable way (how much money your contributions made the company, how much new business you brought in . . . you get the point).

And don't forget entrepreneurialism as a career option. There, by its very nature, success and failure are refreshingly clear. Is there a market for your product? Is it selling? Do you have repeat clients? When you work for yourself, not only is it clear what success looks like, but you get to decide the metrics that define success.

Remember: defined metrics = control. There's power in knowing exactly what your goals are and owning what it will take to achieve them.

CHAPTER 4

The Obligatory Ask-for-the-Raise and How-to-Negotiate Chapter (with a Twist)

You knew this was coming, right?

You just can't have a book like this one without a chapter on negotiating and getting a raise. Heck, there are entire books—okay, an entire cottage industry[1]—on how to ask for a raise.

So that ground is well covered. I won't rehash much of that, don't worry.

Here you may be noting that I spent the whole first part of this book saying that we women should be allowed to act like ourselves, and that we shouldn't have to act like guys to be successful. Yup, I made a pretty big deal about it. And asking for a raise—and negotiating for yourself, and talking about your worth to a company—well, we tend to think of those as guy things.

But bear with me, and I think it will become clear that there's a way to negotiate for those raises—and other things we want—by playing to our strengths rather than playing a part, and making it a win for both sides.

First, let me ask you a question that I always ask whenever I talk to my old crowd, financial advisors: what is a woman's most significant asset?

Sometimes they answer "her equity portfolio"; others say "her house."

The right answer? Herself.

Early in our careers, our future earnings stream[*]—the salaries and bonuses we will earn over the span of our careers—dwarfs our other financial assets. Over time, our other financial assets grow as we save and invest, while at the same time our future earnings stream declines as we approach retirement.

But here's the thing. The more money we make in salaries and bonuses early on in our careers, the higher our future earnings stream is (that is, the more we stand to earn over the long run), as each incremental raise has an accruing effect in the next year and the next and the next and the next. Think about it this way. A woman who starts with a $50,000 a year salary and receives a 3 percent raise each year will end up with a salary of $117,828 after 30 years. But a woman who starts with $50,000 and receives a 5 percent raise every year—just 2 percent higher—will be making $205,807 after 30 years (and this isn't counting bonuses or any other performance-based raises).

So, through much of our career, what is one of the best investments that we women can make? Asking for a raise.

And just for fun, let's think about what would happen if we got an even bigger raise, a raise that (yes, I'm going there) has us making the same salary for the exact same work as a man. Think about it. If we women earn 78 cents to a man's dollar today, then a raise to that dollar earns us a 28 percent return. And it's not just a 28 percent return in that one year; that raise boosts our earnings the next year and the next and the next and the next.

Put another way, if you are earning $85,000 a year today and you get that 28 percent raise, to a guy's level, over 40 years

---

[*] Technically, the net present value of our future earnings stream, for you finance types.

that difference adds up to an additional $1.1 million. That's right: $1.1 million.[2]

This is what I was talking about when I discussed how we can have outsize returns for not-much-more work. Another $1.1 million is an amazing house. Heck, it's an amazing beach house. With a water view. Better yet, that $1.1 million is freedom. Security. The peace of mind that comes with knowing that you will be able to send your kids to college, or help care for your aging parents, and/or retire comfortably.

Don't find it compelling yet? Still feel uncomfortable with the idea of asking for a raise?

Well, there's something else you need to keep in mind about what happens if you don't.

In all the years that I have managed people, the men almost always told me how much money they wanted to make every year. Almost always. I used to joke that they wore a path in the carpet to my office right before bonus time.

The women never did. And by never, I mean never. Never ever. And it matters.

Say we've got two employees, Joe and Joanne. They've both done the same great job this past year; they're both valued workers. They're both set to make the exact same $5,000 bonus.

Joe comes into my office for our weekly catch-up. At the end of it, he says, "I just want to quickly run down a few of my accomplishments this year." He lists them, and then goes on to say, "And I'd like to make $10,000 as a bonus this year."

After Joe leaves, I call my head of human resources to my office. I relay the conversation and we laugh a bit. "Men!" we may chuckle.

Fast-forward to the time to allocate the bonuses. Joe is in for $5,000; we know he wants $10,000. We begin to write down $5,000, but . . .

We don't want to lose Joe, particularly with a big project

coming up. . . . He brought up a couple of accomplishments I had forgotten about. . . . And did you notice that he was on the phone with his door closed the other day? His door is never closed. And isn't the competitor down the street looking for someone with his qualifications?

We really don't want to lose Joe. And we really don't want to upset Joe. And so we put him in for a $7,000 bonus. (We also say that we'll remember next year that we bumped him up this year and smooth it out. But you know we never remember that next year, right?)

Okay, so Joe makes $7,000.

And now Joanne, who's been working just as hard and doing just as well but never asked for any extra money. How much does Joanne make?

When I ask this, the answer I almost always get is $5,000.

Wrong.

Joanne makes $3,000.

Huh?

That's because the money is being allocated out of a bonus pool. The bonus pool is $10,000, and it doesn't grow just because I reallocate it.* In other words, by not asking for that money, you aren't just leaving money on the table: you are essentially handing that money straight over to the guy who *did* ask for the raise or bonus (and trust me, it will be a guy).

'Nuff said. Ask for the friggin' raise.

In the past, the next question was always how much to ask for, and we were essentially flying blind. Plus, it's so awkward to ask your friends what they make. This is where technology helps us—and will help us even more in the future, as start-ups bring in-

---

* I'm using bonuses in this example. Feel free to substitute the word *salary.* Same line of reasoning. You still gotta ask.

creasing transparency to this topic. As I mentioned earlier, check out sites like Comparably.com and Hired.com.

So the question remains: how to ask for that raise? Is the answer that we simply "man up," so to speak, before we head into a negotiation?

I think you know the answer here. For most women, doing this the old way—the man's way—doesn't generally work. That's in part because the hard truth is that (and data supports this) our taking that type of tough approach can backfire for us, as the old gender norms kick in and we are perceived as "bitchy" or "not team players."[3] In addition, it's not really how we're "wired." The research tells us that when men negotiate, they focus on the short-term—i.e., "winning;" when women negotiate, we focus on the long-term—i.e., preserving the relationship after the negotiations are done.[4] (I know this is 100 percent true for me. I hate making job offers; even after all these years and all the job offers I've made, I still have an almost physical aversion to doing it, for fear that the person on the other side of the table will "get mad" at me that the compensation is not generous enough. I know ... seriously, right?)

I also think that this traditional view of negotiating—you ask for the raise and you either get it or you don't—does us a disservice, because it can limit the outcomes to one where one side "wins" and the other "loses." Too often discussion of "getting the raise" gets boiled down to the singular question: Did you get one or not? But this black-and-white approach can cause us to miss the other opportunities for "win-wins" that open up once we introduce more variables into our negotiations.

I can't stress this enough: Yes, the raise is important. Very important. But it's not always *just* about a raise. There are many, many things that can have value for you as you develop your career—like the opportunity to learn new skills, to travel, to work under a particular person at your company . . . and some can be much easier for your manager to say yes to than money in any given year. For example, even with the compounding effects of the raise we talked about, the opportunity to build your skills may arguably be a more tangible value to you for tomorrow than a salary bump is to you today, because it increases your earning power in the long run.

So if you go in and the only ask you have is a raise, you're selling yourself short. Way short. Because if you get a "no" (and you well may), you leave empty-handed. But if you get a "no" and you have other requests that are of value to you—let's say better health benefits, or more vacation, or work-from-home-Fridays—you can leave with a victory. Perhaps not a complete victory, perhaps a victory that won't add money to your next paycheck, but one that can pay off over time. And your boss also starts getting used to saying yes to you. That matters, too.

So instead of focusing on the black-and-white definition of "winning," as men tend to do, why not play to our strengths when we negotiate?

To get there, let's start by calling BS on the conventional wisdom that women are somehow not "as good" at negotiating as men are. Because the truth is more nuanced than this truism allows. For example, have you ever seen a mother negotiate for her child at school? She is fearless, and it's an awesome thing to behold. This isn't just anecdotal; research shows that when a woman is negotiating for someone else—whether her kids, her sister, her colleague—she is a tougher negotiator than most men.[5]

When we feel nervous or uncomfortable going into negotiations (and believe me, I've been there), we can leverage this tendency of ours by thinking about who else will benefit from whatever we are negotiating for, that is, our families. If it's a raise, we can focus on how that raise will help us put funds toward our kids' college educations, or the portion of it we'll donate to the PTA, or our favorite charity. If it's a more flexible schedule, we can think about how our spouses may like having us home more. With this line of thinking our "mama bear" instinct will kick in, allowing us to negotiate more energetically than if we had been thinking only about ourselves.

Another way we can leverage our relationship focus in negotiations is by changing the orientation going in from "I win and you lose" to one of "how can we problem-solve together." In negotiations with your boss, this means getting clear on your value to the company and talking honestly about what is important to you in the negotiation and why. As I said earlier, it won't always simply be about money; there are plenty of other points of value. Maybe it's a more flexible schedule. Maybe it's an overseas assignment. Maybe it's getting as many different experiences as you possibly can. Maybe it's exposure to new ways of marketing. Maybe it's working on a project for one of the top managers at the company. Maybe you're burnt out and need a sabbatical. Maybe you're bored to tears and need to do something different.

Next, and just as important, you need to put those listening and empathy skills to work to help you understand what *she* values and why she values it. If you took the advice in the last chapter, you probably have a sense of what matters to your company already, because you've put in place metrics for your success. But it's worth asking your boss point-blank, What is important to you?

The goal is to figure out what she might value enough that it's worth a raise or promotion. Is she in need of a certain skill set? Then go get that. Or certain experience? Same. The question you should be asking boils down to, How can I be more valuable to you and the company? The answer might not be as obvious as you think. It might be that they need someone to placate an impossible-to-please client, or someone who can write a press release so they can stop outsourcing publicity, or someone who can represent the company at conferences, or someone who can oversee the new tech project with confidence (something that is pretty much always in huge demand). . . . You get the picture. Find out what it is that the company needs and values, and then be the one to deliver it.

Once both sides understand what matters to the other, then we can talk about where our priorities overlap, and what you can do going forward to provide good value in exchange for what the company wants. This is where our natural strengths as communicators are key. The goal is to communicate not just what your priorities are, but *why they are what they are*, and why you think they're also in the interest of the company. Where guys might typically start with some outrageous-but-not-too-outrageous demand, and then move to the center from there, I find great women negotiators tend to be more up front and transparent about what's important to them, and why.

You may be asking: by being so transparent, do we give up our bargaining chips?

Well, maybe in the short-term way. But I find we get something of more long-term value in return. When we make it about our relationship—and about finding a solution that truly is a win for both parties—in negotiation, we build trust, establish rapport, and learn something about what the person on the other side of the table values, something that will potentially come in handy when the next negotiation rolls around.

I've seen this work in practice firsthand. When Sandy Weill approached me to join Citi, following the research scandals of the early 2000s, I knew I was on the other side of the table from a legendary negotiator. I mean, the guy had probably done more acquisitions in financial services than anyone else on the planet. And he was famous for being tough as nails.

First step: I found out what was important to him. He wanted me to come in and establish the independence of Citi's research business and turn the business around ... and thus get Citi's research scandal off the front page of the newspapers. Just make the pain stop. And so his first offer to me was to lead the research business, making about the same compensation that I had made before. His sales pitch: it's a bigger research business than you run now, and you get to turn it around.

Got it. Now I knew what mattered to him.

And I told him I could do that ... but I wasn't motivated by doing what I was already doing, just bigger. What was important to me was that I stretch my experience into a new area. (That old drive for lifelong learning kicking in!) Oh, and that I make more money. (And here my neck began flushing furiously, but I plowed on.) And that the more money should be commensurate with the increased responsibilities. I provided him with my full compensation history so that we were operating from the same set of facts.

He came back and offered me the job of running not just the research business, but also the much larger Smith Barney wealth management business. And he doubled the money.

Could I have gotten something even better—if I had simply charged in and demanded "money or nothing"? Maybe, maybe not. But careers are long-term games, and I've found that this collaborative approach all but guarantees that I come out a winner because people are more likely to want to do business with me again.

CHAPTER 5

Out with the Queen Bee. In with New Approaches to Mentoring and Sponsorship

Have you ever been queen bee'd?

If you are a businesswoman of my generation, the answer is very often yes, meaning that you have come across a more senior woman in the course of your career who didn't support you or, worse, undermined you. And it's a killer. Now, to be fair, her actions were understandable in the context of the business world of her time. Still not cool, but understandable. (More on this in a bit.)

But that world is changing, so now it's time to put a stop to that behavior and break the vicious cycle.

We're going to get to how in a minute. But let's start with playing a little offense. Let's look at some new takes on some old work strategies—on feedback, on mentors, and on sponsors—and how approaching each of these in some perhaps unexpected ways can position us well against the queen bees and others out there holding us back.

Now, we're not naturally born knowing how to be leaders. Instead, leadership is a skill that is built as the result of thousands and thousands of micro-lessons over the course of a career. We most often think of those lessons as provided by a combination of explicit feedback (such as the year-end review) and unspoken feedback (like when the audience talks over your presentation). As we pay attention to this feedback—or better yet, actively seek it out—this helps us grow and improve. But the real leadership lessons don't just come from official performance reviews and embarrassing setbacks. They also happen constantly in office hallways, around proverbial watercoolers, and, increasingly, online.

Stand around a traditional workplace for a while and you can watch it in action: "Hey, Joe, good job on that presentation. Next time be sure to . . ." Or "Hey, Jim, you really stunk it up in there, huh? Next time try . . ."

The thing is, we women receive less of this casual but explicit micro-feedback at work than men do. A lot less. We get less of the "adjust this a tenth of a degree this way" or "try to change this slightly that way" and often more of the implicit feedback—like being left out of an important departmental decision, or not being tapped to participate in a critical project, or being passed over for a promotion or job. The problem is that this kind of feedback doesn't give us much actionable information to work from.

Why are we at this disadvantage?

It's because men remain in the majority of leadership roles, and research shows that they are nervous about women's responses to their explicit feedback. Yes, you guessed it: they are scared we're going to cry.[1]

So what should we do?

Well, first of all, don't cry (or, if you must, take it to the ladies' room . . . fast). Feedback is a gift, even if it can sometimes be hard to hear.

Second, ask for feedback all the time. Then ask for more.

I learned the power of actively—and persistently—soliciting feedback early in my career as a new research analyst. Speaking at the morning meetings, each time I would get up to speak, the most senior analyst, who would always sit right in the front row, would sigh—very loudly—and simultaneously place his head in his hands and shake it from side to side. It was not only demoralizing but also humiliating, because if you were a member of the sales force looking at me talking at the morning meeting, you also had a direct view of him, sighing and shaking his head. (Be assured, I am not exaggerating this in the least.) Yes, it got under my skin; my voice would shake and my saliva would disappear.

It might have been funny if it weren't my career we were talking about.

After a few days of this, I gathered up my courage and went into this guy's office and asked him for some feedback on my performance. As you might imagine, he declined to give any; he said it wasn't his job. (I know, with someone like that, what did I really expect?)

But I felt like my career was on the line, so I didn't let it die there; I started asking for feedback from everyone else. How could I improve how I performed in the morning meeting? Did I make a cogent case for my stock recommendation? Did they see holes in my argument?

I found that the first time I asked someone these questions, I generally got a "You're doing great." The second time I asked I would get a slightly less emphatic "Really, you're fine." But here's the key: the third time, the person would generally start to recognize that I really wanted to improve and would finally say something I could use.

Eventually, one analyst came through with "Don't let your voice lilt up at the end of a sentence. It makes you sound like a little kid, and you lose credibility."

Oof. It stung a bit to hear that, but it was also incredibly helpful. Advice like this might sound insignificant (and no, it's not right and it's not fair that something like that could matter, but it did), but overnight I changed the way I spoke in meetings in such a way that I sounded more mature. I tried to convey as much of that all-important gravitas as I could muster.

While this may seem like a little thing, it may have been the best feedback I've ever received. If my voice was getting in the way of my message, that was valuable information. And having the knowledge gave me the ability to change it, to make sure I was heard. In fact, it's the accumulation of seemingly minor tips and points like this that can make the difference between blissfully unaware mediocrity and growing into a real leader.

To this day, I still ask for feedback all the time from everyone: bosses, employees, peers. And, of course, this can also mean that I sometimes receive more "feedback" than I might like. For example, when I announced that I was putting together a team to build Ellevest, we got a lot of feedback. Much of it was encouraging, but some of it was the prediction that we were doomed to fail; others had failed in trying to build something that works for women, and so we would fall flat on our faces, too, the thinking went. Some of it was the equivalent of saying that women need financial advice that is "dumbed down," so what we were doing was too ambitious. Some of it was that women need more "hand-holding," so what we were doing wasn't traditional enough.

Clearly not all feedback is created equal. So this raises the question of how to prioritize and parse through feedback. How should one decide what to take to heart and what to ignore?

My thoughts on this: listen to the critics and ignore the cynics.

First, let's talk about the critics: yes, what they say may be tough to hear, but they're worth listening to. These people may have been in your shoes before. They probably care about what you are trying to do. They likely operate from a place of trying to make you—and what you are building—better. Otherwise they would just tell you "you're fine," which is often a hell of a lot easier than telling you what you need to do to improve. They may even have emotional skin in the game. My fellow research analysts at Bernstein (again, besides the head-shaking, loud-sighing guy) often told me that my getting better at my job was only good for them, since it made the whole department better. And so when they criticized my work, it came from a genuine place of wanting us all to prosper.

The cynics? You can recognize them because they've *always* got something negative to say, even, or sometimes especially, if you're killing it (that goes double for the queen bee, but more on that in a minute). They seem to revel in people failing. They seem to think your success might somehow detract from their own, and so they feel threatened. I've also noticed they tend to be the ones making their comments into a computer keyboard as opposed to face-to-face. If you get a long snarky email or tweet time-stamped 1 a.m., odds are you're dealing with a cynic.

Listen to the critics; invite feedback from the critics; thank the critics. Ignore the cynics.

This brings us to the worst kind of cynic women can face ... the queen bee. She is one kind of cynic that can really knock us off our game.

She's the woman who has been successful, but she seems allergic to doing anything to help other women reach the top. She's the one who says, "If I had to do it the hard way, so should you." She's the one who knocks the ladder out from behind her.

Yes, mean girls do exist after high school. But sometimes they can be hard to spot. Male bullies tend to yell, but as the *Harvard Business Review*[2] writes, women tend to sabotage one another more subtly. It's called "relational aggression," and it will feel very familiar to those of us who were blindsided by the dazzling viciousness of mean girls when we were younger. There are countless scenarios for how bullying between women plays out,[3] but in the workplace it often involves you being gossiped about or cut out of a project.

Despite the fact that the Workplace Bullying Institute[4] labels "woman-on-woman" bullying with a cheerful acronym— WOW!—they acknowledge it as a major problem for women at work, noting that, even though there are more male than female bullies, women are more likely to target other women than to target men. Ironically, this is particularly true in macho workplaces where the few women there can be subtly encouraged to turn on one another.

Speak to senior businesswomen of my generation and they've all got a story about female peers who were less than supportive along the way.

I was queen bee'd once, big-time, and it was one of the nastiest surprises of my professional life. A senior woman told me she would advise me in navigating a tricky professional situation (I still have the notes I took on the phone call when she said she would guide me through it) and that I could count on her. Then I began to hear through the grapevine that she was telling other people that she didn't like it when I had done X and she didn't like my presentation on Y and she had vetoed my speaking at the Z conference (to which I had been invited) because she wanted to speak at it instead. I honestly felt like the sophomore in high school who had upset the head of the cheerleading squad. But because the vibes were coming to me through the grapevine, and because she continued to advise me and say she was my biggest supporter, I struggled with how to deal with it. Should I try to discuss this with her? Or take her at her word?

I didn't have that dilemma for long. Soon my supposed "biggest supporter" was one of the people on the other side of the table from me when I was reorganized out of the company.

Now why the heck do women do this to each other?

Often the queen bee acts this way because she feels threatened; she sees you as competition for one of the (woefully) few places for women at the top. And to be brutally honest, as I was making my way up the ladder on Wall Street, the women there all sort of knew—without ever saying the words—that there would really only ever be one or two seats for a woman at the senior management table. So if you were there, and you weren't ready to give yours up . . . well, you get the picture.

Other times she may just be replaying—consciously or not—how another queen bee treated her at some point in her career. The psychotherapist Phyllis Chesler wrote a whole book, *Women's Inhumanity to Women*,[5] about how we sometimes reenact what's been done to us by a sexist world.

There may be another reason. Recent research shows that, in general, we tend to be compassionate to others when they go through difficult times. But if the difficult situation they are experiencing is something that *we also have been through,* we become less compassionate.[6] We are more "Buck up" than "Let me help you." Many times I've heard, "Well, I had to fight my way up the corporate ladder the hard way; so should she."

There may also be another, perhaps more disturbing reason. A University of Colorado study[7] showed that women and people of color who have advocated for women and people of color, respectively, have historically been penalized for it. (The slight good news is that, in contrast, Caucasian men receive a reputation bump from advocating for those same two groups.)

Whatever the reason for queen beeing, it needs to stop. The first step is recognizing that the (business) pie can grow. And thus there can be more seats at the table. That's what the changes in business we talked about in the first chapter and the rise in entrepreneurialism mean. Our options have exploded, and it's no longer winner-take-all, at all. And we need to recognize that women helping one another get ahead is good for each of us (and, remember, good for the economy and society and our families).

Once this is understood, we can call out the queen bee when we see her. We can confront her face-to-face about her behavior. It's important to call her out if it's happening to you. And it's even more important to call it out if we see it happening to others. Her negative energy is toxic for everyone in the workplace, and it shouldn't be tolerated.

Okay, now that we've killed off the queen bee, what's next? Well, what's the opposite of the queen bee? It's women making a commitment to help other women get ahead.

So not only should we invest our time in asking for feedback; it's also important that we invest our time in *giving* feedback—especially to other women.

Personally, I don't love giving feedback. Like so many of us, I'm all about preserving the relationship, so my first inclination is to keep the waters smooth. After all, I don't want to ruffle feathers or upset anyone.

But that's shortsighted of me. And so I have worked to master the art of the "stick and move." That's what I call quick feedback, delivered in a matter-of-fact, no-big-deal voice. And then off to the next topic. No trying to make sure that the other person is okay with getting the feedback, no long exposition on the ways in which the other person is doing a great job, no reaffirming how much I like the person, no apologizing for the feedback. Just stick and move. Like ripping off a Band-Aid.

The natural next step to getting and receiving feedback is letting a mentorship relationship evolve. Now, the word *mentor* used to make me feel almost like I was going to break out in hives. That's probably because I participated in one too many corporate mentoring programs in which I would be paired with another female professional. She would come to my office at the appointed time with a list of questions written down on her pad of paper. She would read them off to me robotically and I would answer them, while praying the clock magically would speed up. And we would both be relieved when our time together was over.

Much more valuable than these HR-mandated exercises in

sometimes mutual awkwardness are the mentoring relationships that develop naturally between people who respect each other's work. That can easily happen as an outgrowth of all of the feedback we are asking for and receiving. Or it can simply emerge because we happen to respect each other.

We women have actually gotten pretty good at the mentor thing. But that's not enough. You need "sponsors" as well: those individuals who not only answer your questions but also advocate for you. The Center for Talent Innovation estimates that women have three times as many mentors as men but that men are 46 percent more likely to have sponsors.[8]

How important are sponsors? Two stories:

The first: Back at Bernstein, as I was asking for all of that feedback, the senior property casualty insurance analyst, Weston Hicks, took me under his wing. He read every piece of my research and critiqued it. He argued my reasoning on upgrading and downgrading stocks with me. He fought to get my research published when I was at a more junior level than was typically allowed. He pushed for me to get a promotion. He introduced me to his clients and recommended that they read my research. He fought for me. And I never forgot it.

His constructive criticism was at times hard to hear, but it was worth it. Thanks to his guidance I was more successful and got ahead more quickly than I would have without it. On this there is no doubt in my mind. In fact, there was another research analyst with a more analytical background than mine and with more direct experience who started at Bernstein at about the same time as I and didn't have Weston as a sponsor. I made it into a ranked analyst position (that is, I was voted by clients as one of the top analysts in my area of coverage) a full two years before the other analyst did. Thus I would argue that the sponsorship relationship took two years off my career trajectory. At least.

Relationships like this are a virtuous cycle. As Sylvia Ann

Hewlett points out, a successful relationship like that does not stay one-way for forever. As I got my research analyst legs under me, I was able to critique Weston's research, too, so the relationship also benefited him (I think) and grew that much stronger as a result.

When I did not have a critical sponsor like this in place—and when I was therefore navigating my career on my own—the results were completely different.

I've spoken about how I was reorganized out of Bank of America, where I ran Merrill Lynch. But the story doesn't stop there. On the first night home after I'd been reorgnanized, I hit the wine bottle. Pretty hard, actually. (Can you blame me?) On the first full day after it, I camped on my sofa, in my sweatpants, feeling sort of tender and sorry for myself.

On the second day, I decided I didn't want to let the opportunity pass to learn from what had just happened, particularly while it was fresh. So I reached out to members of the board of directors with two messages. The first: "Thank you for giving me the opportunity to run Merrill Lynch. It was a real honor." The second: "What could I have done better?"

Each one who would return my call said essentially the same thing: "You didn't have anyone fighting for you." In other words: no support. No sponsor in that room.

Now, to be perfectly clear, the business I ran was ahead of plan, it was the only business at the company that was growing, and it was gaining share. But without someone in that room advocating for me—saying "Not her. Let's not terminate her. Let's terminate someone who's missing plan"—I was out on my ear.

And this is when I began to *really* "get" the power of these relationships. First, my (outside of Bank of America) sponsors sprang into action. As I navigated those early days after my firing, full of questions—Should I jump back into a corporate job right away? Should I go into a regulatory role? Should I take on a board position?—these people, with their differing ideas and perspectives, were invaluable to me, even when they weren't saying exactly what I wanted to hear. Actually, that made them even more valuable, because I knew that my judgment was likely a bit off after the blow of being fired.

That's when I began to think of this group as being my own personal board of directors.

So what are the lessons?

There are ones you already know: mentors matter; sponsors matter more.

But it's more than that. The amazing Carla Harris—who has combined an ultra successful career on Wall Street with a side avocation of gospel singing—has noted that "[a]ll the important decisions about your career take place when you're not in the room." That's true for promotions, for raises, for decisions about funding you, whether to engage you for a project, whether to buy from you, what valuation to offer you on a deal.

So, ask yourself, *Who is in that room? And who is in that room fighting for me?*

That's where the feedback is so valuable, where having the mentors guiding you is so valuable—and where having the sponsor is so invaluable.

That's why, while thinking through what to do next after being tossed out of Bank of America, I decided to make a concerted effort to mentor a handful of women entrepreneurs in New York. I believed I would be able to help them, and I would be able to make some connections for them that could help their businesses.

The surprise was that, without my even knowing what the words meant, they quickly "reverse mentored" me. So while I was making connections for them and guiding them in some corporate introductions, for example, I was learning from them about entrepreneurialism and social media and what was on the minds of women their age.

Maybe you already know all of this. Maybe my experiences just underscore this for you.

But here's what else we all should be doing to make real progress: When you're in that room—and, if you do things right, you will make it into that room—and the future of another deserving woman is being discussed, how about you do this? How about you fully reject the way of the queen bee, and show your support? How about you don't hang back? Instead speak up about all the things this woman has done well (assuming she has, of course) and why she should be given the raise or the bonus or the promotion. Acknowledge the research finding that a woman supporting another woman is typically discounted. (This is key, because this will have the effect of sensitizing everyone to this gender bias and thus take it right off the table.) And then tell 'em why Joanie is great, why Susan is the one for the job, why Samantha can get the job done. Be their champion.

People will listen to you. And not only will it help Joanie, and Susan, and Samantha, it will also position you as a true leader. Done this way, it will enhance your reputation. It can transform the way others around that table see you.

Now, if only one of us does this, it probably won't make a lot of difference. If all of us do this, it will make all the difference. If the queen bee held womankind back, being a sponsor, the anti–queen bee, can move us forward.

CHAPTER 6

. . . Oh, and Some Thoughts on How to Do the Networking Thing Better, Too

We've talked about mentoring and sponsoring, so you know what's coming next: networking. I know, I know, you've heard all about the importance of networking before. But we need to talk about it and I hope to share some insights you *haven't* heard. Because it matters.

Since I graduated from business school, I've worked at four companies, I've been on four for-profit boards, I've been on six nonprofit boards, I've found one cofounder, I've found one president of Ellevate Network, I've invested in one joint venture, and I've bought one business. None of those connections has been made through a search firm; all of them have been through my network.

A few years ago, I bought the then cheekily named 85 Broads (now Ellevate Network), the professional women's network with roots at Goldman Sachs. How that happened is a great illustration of the power of networks.

It started when I happened to be seated on a plane next to the former chairman of the Securities and Exchange Commission, Arthur Levitt. As I recall, I turned to him and said, "You're

Arthur Levitt!" And, as I also recall, he turned back to me and said, "And you're . . . ?"

"Sallie Krawcheck!" I said. "I'm Sallie Krawcheck!"

We had both worked with Sandy Weill at various points in our careers, and so (once I introduced myself) we had plenty to talk about on that flight. We kept in touch for the next few years.

When I left Bank of America, Arthur reached out to me and said, "I know someone who wants to meet you." So connection number one introduced me to connection number two, a banker at Goldman Sachs . . . who introduced me to (connection three) an entrepreneur . . . who introduced me to (four) a venture capitalist . . . who introduced me to (five) the former head of a research firm . . . who introduced me to (six) another entrepreneur . . . who introduced me to (seven) the CEO of General Assembly . . . who introduced me to (eight) a young entrepreneur wannabe . . . who introduced me to (nine) the owner of 85 Broads.

Nine introductions, over several years, got me to the place where I met the founder of 85 Broads.

(While I'm at it, number 8 also introduced me to another entrepreneur, number 10, who introduced me to my Ellevest cofounder, number 11.)

It's examples like these that demonstrate why women report that networking is the number one unwritten rule of success in business.[1] In particular, entrepreneurs—and even more specifically, female entrepreneurs—report that their network can be absolutely key for the success of their start-up.

That said, I can't tell you how many women—and especially young women—tell me they think networking is "cheating," that they want to do it "on their own."

Yeah . . . that's not how it works. I wonder if this was the lesson we took away from all those fairy tales fed to us as little girls: Sleeping Beauty, Cinderella, Snow White. They told us that if we did the right things and kept quiet, our prince would come, often aided by a fairy godmother. Newsflash: the princes are all busy at the bar handing out business cards to their future bosses, and fairy godmothers don't work in human resources. Please network.

But it's not just enough to network; what matters is with whom and how you network. I can't tell you how many young women report to me that they conflate networking with making friends. Of the eleven people who played a part in my journey to buy Ellevate Network, I like each of them. I am more than happy to have a glass of wine with any and all of them. I'm friendly with them. But I'm not *friends* with any of them. I don't think any of them could tell you the names of my children or me theirs. But taken together, they changed my life.

The truth is that your next business connection is far more likely to come from someone you barely know—a loose connection—than from a friend or close connection. I used to joke that my friends would never give me a business opportunity because they knew me too well. But, really, it's because you and your friends, and your work colleagues, and the people you speak to all the time, tend to traffic in the same connections and information. It's only by pulling in the knowledge of individuals who are steps away from you that you learn about the board position that you didn't know was open, the talented young person looking for the job, the start-up that is threatening yours, the research that you should really read.

I've seen us women (men, too, but mostly women) make a lot of the same networking mistakes. The number one mistake, of course, is not networking. This one is particularly common among women in their thirties. Life is busy, after all. Maybe you're building a new relationship with a spouse or partner, you have young kids, the job is all-consuming, and all the while you're trying to keep up with friends, and you have some great shows lined up on

Netflix. You know you *should* go to that industry cocktail hour—but then you imagine putting on Spanx and standing around awkwardly drinking chardonnay and talking business with strangers . . . well, it never makes it to number one on your list. I get it. Believe me, I get it.

But our thirties—once we've all proven that we're good at our jobs—is exactly when networking becomes that much *more* valuable. This is the time where the guys' network is one of the key reasons they can move past us at work. They *are* going to the cocktail parties (minus the Spanx . . . I think), which means they learn about the opportunities that we might not; they meet the decision makers; they simply get to know more people. If we've taken time off to have kids, networking is all the more vital, as we're playing catch-up (and can be all the harder, because going out and meeting new people usually means missing a few bedtimes).

So remember that showing up counts. For making initial connections, nothing beats actual in-person events. Maybe a friend of a friend of a friend of a friend got a great job on LinkedIn through a random request to connect. But this is a pretty low-return undertaking. Go out. This doesn't mean you have to accept every invitation; choose the events you feel will deliver the highest return, put them on your calendar weeks in advance, and then don't cancel or bail. Simple as that.

The second mistake I see women make is rushing it. Networks are like any good investment portfolio. The great ones can have an extremely high ROI (return on investment), but not right away, and often not from the sources that one might expect. Of course, we ladies intuitively get this since we are wired to look at the long term. But when we try to contort ourselves to network the "man's way" it's easy to forget that professional relationships, like any other, don't sprout out of the ground overnight, fully formed. They need tending, nurturing—and that takes time.

This brings me to the third mistake so many women make when networking: not following up with people they meet. We can put our natural strengths as relationship builders to good use here. Once a relationship with someone is established, for goodness' sake, stay in touch or—as I call it—"play in traffic." Otherwise, out of sight may be out of mind. I can't tell you how many times I've run into someone and they did the old "slap the head with the hand" thing and said, "Oh, man. I just heard of a project you would have been perfect for, but I referred it to someone else," or "Darn it, I just recommended someone else for a board position that could have made a whole lot of sense for you." This would not have happened if I had stayed in better touch.

How do you play in traffic? Well, some of it still involves going out. But this is an area in which technology can become your friend: the quick text message check-in with someone, the email making an introduction, the tweet linking to an article they might find interesting. So following up doesn't have to be time-consuming; it should be purposeful, though.

Another mistake: so many people end up only networking in their own company. That's important, but by itself, too limiting. Way too limiting. How else are you going to get a view of the competitive landscape, the open jobs, the emerging start-ups, the talented young people looking for jobs, and the advisory council positions if you don't have connections outside your existing company?

I had a pretty strong network at Bank of America. (Okay, no sponsor, obviously, but a pretty strong peer network.) But I can tell you that when I was "restructured out," that network dropped me like a hot potato. Seriously, the number of holiday cards I got from those now-former colleagues declined by about 95 percent.

And I'll never forget a conversation I had with a senior woman there the day after I was given my walking papers. (Not the queen bee. Another woman.) I called her to tell her what a pleasure it had been to work with her and how much I had enjoyed getting to know her. I can still hear her exact words. "Sallie," she said, "I want to keep in touch. I don't want to just say we're going to keep in touch; I really want to keep in touch."

Well, fast-forward to today. She didn't take or return the phone calls I placed to her in the years since. And she wouldn't even accept my LinkedIn request! (Talk about a low-commitment way to keep in touch!)

Listen, I totally get it. People get sort of embarrassed when others are fired or reorganized out; it's awkward. People are busy. People move on; out of sight, out of mind, right? It's completely understandable.

But, boy, that incident sure drove home the point that an external network is key. And, if you're thinking now, *Yes, but I'm not going to get fired*, believe you me, I thought the same thing (and I thought I had the business results to back me up). When the unthinkable happened, my Bank of America colleagues vanished, but thank goodness for that external network that sprang into action, unasked, presenting me with new opportunities.

One final point: waiting to network until you need that network is like waiting to save for retirement till the day you retire. You're doomed.

So whatever it is you are currently doing now, and whether you are employed or not, start networking now, both within and outside of your company.

How much do I believe in the power of networking?

When I was a kid, there was a TV commercial for a Remington electric shaver, featuring an entrepreneur named Victor Kiam. In it he said, "I liked the shaver so much, I bought the company." Well, I believe in networking so much that I bought a professional network. And, as noted in the last chapter, I believe in the power of women helping women—and the power of women networking with women—so much that I made sure it was a women's network.

Ellevate Network began its life as the informal women's alumni network for Goldman Sachs and has now grown to tens of thousands of women strong, across industries and around the world. Seeing these professional women who are rewriting the rules of business get together and support one another is just about one of my favorite things in life. At my very first Ellevate networking event, I witnessed two women give another woman, who had just lost her job, a handful of leads; another two shared resources for a special needs child; and a third group helped another dissect a recent performance review. And there was wine! Now, that's networking.

Should we network with women? You know it. I have found that we can understand one another's experiences—and thus support one another and cheer one another on—in a way those who don't have those shared experiences can't. And I love nothing more than helping to put another crack in the glass ceiling by sharing the information that can help another woman get ahead.

Should we network with guys, too? Absolutely. And, in fact, since they hold more positions of power (for the time being), it's crucial.

Remember to be patient. The new contacts you make likely won't find you a new job or get you a big deal next week. (I almost don't know how to reply to the email sitting in my inbox from a female entrepreneur lamenting that she keeps trying to sell her new product to people she's just added to her network, but they won't buy . . . or even reply.) But over time, any one of your new contacts can provide a strong return. And in the meantime, meeting smart, interesting people will not only help you see new perspectives, learn new things, and open you up to new career opportunities—it can also be a source of well-earned fun.

Here are my four core rules of networking:

1. I try to meet at least one new person in my area of interest every month, or significantly deepen an existing relationship.

2. I do something nice for someone in my network every week. It doesn't have to be a big find-someone-a-job favor, but instead can be connecting two people who should know each other, sharing research or information that someone you know may find useful, or posting a LinkedIn recommendation on a colleague.

3. I make sure that I am spending time with professionals who are different from me. At an extreme, if my network is made up solely of female financial services professionals of my generation, who all hail from the South, I will likely feel very comfortable with them. And I will likely enjoy my time with them. And I will no doubt learn from them. But at some point, this will become an echo chamber of similar-enough experiences and perspectives.

4. When people don't return my phone calls or emails I apply the MRI ("most respectful interpretation") of their not returning the call, and don't take it personally. I reach out again a week or two later. And if they still don't get back to me, well, their loss, right? There are plenty of fish in the sea.

So do yourself a favor. Find at least one hour each week to network, in person. Call the babysitter, duck out of work early, skip just this one Spin class. Whatever you have to do to find the time, find it. Trust me, in the long run, it's worth it.

CHAPTER 7

Career Curveballs—Why We Really Need to Get Over Our Fear of the F-Word

Failure. Ugh. Downer. Who wants to talk about failure?

Not us women. We love to get our A's, remember?

Failure can be terrifying, no doubt about it. And our fear of the F-word starts at a young age; research shows that girls are more likely to see failure as a sign that they are inherently deficient in some way, whereas boys see it as a result of circumstance.[1] And it may be because it's part of the messaging we receive from our parents and from society, as Girls Who Code founder Reshma Saujani pointed out in her 2016 TED Talk: that while boys are taught to be brave, girls are taught to be perfect.[2]

This quest for perfection stays with us when we're older, and it holds us back. A 2014 *Time* magazine[3] article reported on a poll that revealed that females' "unwillingness to fail, or a fear of doing anything that could lead to a washout might be one of the pinch-points that is impeding women's progress to the head office."

This certainly lines up with what I've seen in my career. Because for all the talk in business about the benefits of embracing failure, failing fast, failing early ... failure is still so ... you know ... embarrassing for many of us. And particularly for us women.

But it's important that we have honest conversations about failure, because the lessons from it are so powerful, especially given the rapidly changing world of work.

Many of us aren't having these honest discussions. It wasn't so long ago that I had breakfast with a friend who was pretty widely known to have been fired from her senior job in media. I went into the breakfast armed with a list of potential contacts and business opportunities for her. I was ready not only to commiserate (hey, I've been there) but also to help. Instead she took immediate control of the conversation and walked me through all the reasons why she had *not* been fired. I think I lived through her "not getting fired" in real time, reliving it conversation by conversation with her boss. It was frustrating for me because honestly, I simply didn't care what the circumstances of her leaving were, and it took time away from our strategizing her next move.

So, why does learning to fail matter so much?

Because it's going to happen no matter what. The business world is changing so fast that encountering career curveballs along the way is inevitable. Simply inevitable. Only resilience, built up through failing, talking openly and honestly about failing, and overcoming failing, will win the day. In fact, in a recent survey[4] by Accenture, 71 percent of corporate leaders around the world reported that resilience is "very to extremely important" in deciding which employees to keep on. These same corporate leaders also associate resilience with seniority, with 77 percent saying senior managers are the most resilient members of their teams. So, whether resilience is the chicken and success is the egg or vice versa (does resilience make you more successful? or does success mean you become more resilient?) is irrelevant: these two are becoming more like peas and carrots—they go together.

The truth is—and though it can be tough to admit it for us perfectionistic women—failure can be a gift, because it brings with it enormous information. Was it that we had the wrong skill set?

Was management looking for a fresh perspective? Were we the victim of office politics? Is the business changing in a way that's moving away from us? In many cases, it's likely it was some combination of a number of these things. (And because there may not be one obvious, clear-cut reason we fail—usually it's the interplay of multiple factors—this is where our natural ability to deal with complexity comes in handy; the old weighing-all-the-menu-items trick.)

We all fail. And we're all going to fail in the future. We're going to fail if we're taking chances, such as going for the promotion or the raise. And we're certainly going to face increased chances of failing if we start our own businesses.

I am fortunate that I got comfortable with failing early. My research analyst job was all about making stock recommendations, based on what was, by definition, imperfect information. And as you read earlier, I made those recommendations in public. So when I failed, I failed in front of everyone. With no one to blame but myself.

I'll never forget almost sinking through the floor when a client called one day to tell me he had caught a math error in one of my reports. I started to make excuses, to bluster that it wasn't a mistake. But of course he was right. So I stopped, thanked him for finding it, tried to think of other people to blame for a minute, and then proverbially kicked myself in the rear.

But that experience didn't kill me. And in fact his having caught it—and his giving me the courtesy of bringing it to my attention—served only to make my research, and my fact-checking process, better. This taught me quickly that failure is not fatal.

I've written about my firing at Citi. That was tough. But in many ways, being "reorganized out" of Bank of America was tougher. As I mentioned, the CEO who had hired me left soon after, and I never made it into the new CEO's inner circle. There was no easy rapport between us, and I only learned about what was going on at the company when the rest of the company learned about it, which, believe me, is a clear warning sign at a senior level. I told my team, let's just make sure we make our (proverbial) A's; let's run the business the right way, let's make our plan, let's be the least of his problems.

On the day after Labor Day 2011, the business was in good shape. We were 13½ percent ahead of plan, which is a lot for a wealth management business. We were gaining share versus our competitors. And ours was the only business at the company that was growing. More important, we had achieved what we had set out to do, which was to lower the financial advisor attrition from about the 50 percent level (!), at which it was running when I was brought in, to the single digits.

I remember sitting in a meeting—it was about 2:45 p.m.—when my assistant brought me a note that the CEO wanted to see me at 3:30. As I walked back to my office before going to see him, I had the sinking feeling I was about to be fired.

When I told my longtime assistant this, "No, you're not" was her startled response. But the fact that the CEO and I didn't have a "Hey, why don't you swing by my office so that we can bat around a couple of ideas?" kind of relationship helped me recognize that this was an important (read: ominous) meeting.

As I limped over to his office—I had a stress fracture in my foot and so was wearing one of those awkward broken-foot boots—I passed the company's head of commercial banking. This guy was probably the biggest "Hey, how's everybody doing?" backslapper I've ever met. Booming voice. Lots of compliments for everyone all the time. A 100 percent extrovert. But when I walked by him this time, there was no backslapping. No question about how my Labor Day was. Or whether my kids had had a nice summer. No sympathetic comment on my (incredibly obvious) injury. Just a mumbled hello while he looked at his own slightly more stylish shoes.

I knew I was doomed. Cue the *Jaws* music again.

Elsewhere in the building, my team was already being assembled for a dinner, to be led by that same commercial banking head, during which they would discuss the new Sallie-less business structure. The press release about my exit had already been prepared ... and they released it twenty minutes after I left the CEO's office. They put the announcement out so quickly that I didn't even have time to tell my family; my father found out when he looked up from the couch and saw it on CNBC. (Ouch.)

Major career curveball.

I went home; I drank wine. And then I drank some more wine.

As I reflected on a few of the departmental moves that the CEO had made over the summer, it was clear this had been in the works for a while. Yet the whole thing, while not a complete surprise, still felt like a random act of violence. And it seemed like a gross insult to my long-held values system: work hard, deliver results, succeed. (And, seriously, if they were planning for it for a while, they couldn't have done it in July, and given me the summer with the kids? They had to do it the *day after Labor Day*? What kind of monsters were those people??!!)

This go-round felt in many ways different from my first firing from Citi, which had been brought on by a fundamental business disagreement. But they did have some things in common. Each was, at its heart, driven by change: change that happened beyond my control. In each case there had been a change in leadership, which in turn meant a change in office politics, which in turn meant a change in company culture. And those changes were themselves driven by the rapidly changing business environment (think financial crisis).

I've seen it again and again: when managers change, their teams most often change, too. At Citi, I had been hired by Sandy Weill. Less than a year after I started, he informed me that he was retiring, having been exhausted by the NASDAQ market crash of 2000 and its aftereffects. In came Chuck Price as CEO, who was ousted during the early innings of the 2007–08 market crash, giving way to Vikram Pandit. And as the CEOs changed, so did the CEOs' senior teams, and so did the senior teams' teams and their teams and so on. The turnover was so great, in fact, that I was actually the last of Sandy Weill's direct reports left reporting to Vikram Pandit . . . and then there were none.

And the pace of this kind of turnover is only quickening, as markets become more volatile and businesses become more rapidly disrupted. And it doesn't just affect those at the top. Let's take the example of Merrill Lynch. For years and years, there was tremendous leadership continuity . . . until there wasn't. Up to the year 2000, the business had one boss for fifteen years (and that guy spent a total of thirty-eight at the company). But since the NASDAQ meltdown of 2000 and the subprime crisis of 2007–08, Merrill has had eight different head honchos (unless I'm missing someone, which is reasonably likely); that's one about every two years. And each of those leaders tended to establish their own management teams (as new leaders do), and each of those leaders had changes in business strategy (as new leaders do), so the change rippled all the way through the organization.

If you're thinking that this phenomenon is unique to Wall Street, think again. It's happening everywhere: look at technology, look at media, look at marketing, where teams and companies are being shaken up seemingly overnight. These are not just one-offs, and, in my view, it doesn't slow down from here.

Sometimes there may not appear to be much rhyme or reason when one person keeps their job and another doesn't. Sometimes it's random, undeserved, political, or more about circumstances than anything else. Realizing that can help us become more resilient, not just to major curveballs like getting fired, but to smaller ones, too—like getting passed over for a promotion, or losing a big client, or being publicly berated by a boss. These too happen to all of us.

So how do you build resilience against failure?

Part of being truly resilient is making sure you have your "insurance" in place. This includes the kind of peace of mind that money can buy: Did you negotiate for that raise? Did you volunteer for that extra assignment to build your skill set? Did you save the three- to six-month emergency fund that almost every personal finance expert recommends? Did you invest your savings in a diversified investment portfolio (more on this later) so that you built a nest egg to live off of while you look for something else?

Do you have other kinds of "insurance" in place? Is your network strong? Do you have sponsors who can help you think through your next steps?

Have you taken a coding class? Or a finance class? And have you kept your skills fresh? If you do, you'll be in much, much better shape when failure comes along than if you stagnated in your job.

One more thought. When I speak to women, they often bring up something that they also think of as failure: quitting. Maybe it's our risk aversion or long-term focus talking, but I can't tell you how many women I talk to who see quitting as almost akin to being fired. Their boss has passed over them for the promotion, they are not listened to, or they get the cross-eyed look if they leave early to pick up their kid; or maybe they simply weren't finding meaning and purpose in their jobs. In my mind, these can be perfectly legitimate reasons to walk out the door. But when I talk to women like this I so often hear that sense of "it's my fault": "If I had just tried harder to make the relationship with my boss work," or "if we had just talked it through . . ."

Look, sometimes it simply doesn't make sense to keep plugging away at something that doesn't work for us. And there's no shame in that.

Back in the day, when I worked at Salomon Brothers in London, I turned around and recognized—at the ripe age of something like twenty-six—that I was the senior woman in the investment banking department. I had my fair share of being asked to pour the coffee in meetings and assorted other 1980s *Working Girl*-esque clichés.... And at some point I decided that I really didn't think fighting those battles, as an American just a few years out of college in a foreign country, was what I wanted to do. So I quit. I simply quit. And I went on to choose battles that I believed were more winnable.

Here's a final piece of advice for those of us wanting to build resilience in our daughters, our nieces, or the young people we mentor, and this one is a little more out there: get them on the basketball court or on the soccer field or into volleyball. Seriously! Would you believe there's a relationship between a woman's success in business and whether she played competitive sports in school? Amazingly, 96 percent of C-suite women have played team sports.[5] One theory is that, in addition to teaching collaboration, sports force us to face failure and see that failure is not fatal. Key to being successful in sports, as in business, is recognizing that failure is part of the process.

But resilience is not all I learned about failure from the whole Bank of America debacle. I also learned that failure, while sometimes embarrassing, can lead to bigger and better—and more exciting—things, as it did for me after the new CEO shot me. In fact, failing big has been perhaps the luckiest thing in my career. It's not just me saying this. I hear it from many people: failure can actually open doors that you didn't even know were there.

Honestly, I wasn't particularly happy at Bank of America, but I would never have left it had I not been "encouraged" against my will to do so. The business I ran had tens of thousands of people working in it. I felt a responsibility to each of them to get the business turned around and on a healthy footing. So even if I wasn't happy in the job, abandoning my responsibilities just because I felt left out of the "CEO's team" would have seemed to me self-indulgent. (And, truth be told, I simply couldn't imagine calling my father and telling him I had quit because the CEO wasn't very nice to me.)

So even as I sat home the day after that very public "failure," I sort of knew that this was going to open opportunities for me that I never would have had if I had stayed on. Even being given the bum's rush out the door was itself a bit of a gift; it made it awfully hard to wish that I could continue to spend more time with those folks than I did with my family. It was freeing.

I would never ever have embarked on being an entrepreneur if I hadn't been fired. And so I would never have been as completely and totally engaged with my work or have found the sense of real purpose in my work that I have now.

I'm sometimes asked if I was nervous that this firing was "it" for me?

Actually, no, I wasn't. Because I had learned as an analyst that failure isn't "game over." You get as many "at bats" as you choose to take . . . and, let's face it, everyone loves a good comeback story.

That said, I'm not going to deny that failure sucks in the moment. But you can get through it. The way I've done that is through trying to adjust my perspective. I recognize how fortunate I've been in my life.

I think about my good fortune to have been born during this era, to great parents, to have had the education they gave me, to have been economically secure, to have healthy children. In other words, I was lucky to have been given the opportunities to take chances, to chase my ambitions, to make big bets on myself and on my career. And I love the career I've had the good fortune to build, curveballs and all.

Once I recognized this, it put failure in an entirely different context, as something to own and embrace, not run away from. The opportunity to fail in business, I realized, is a gift many are not given.

CHAPTER 8

How to Avoid the Career Risk You Don't Even Know You're Taking

Okay, so now we're (more) comfortable with failing. We're getting past the shame that we can feel; we recognize that failure can teach us a lot; we understand that failure is only going to become more commonplace in the future as the pace of business accelerates.

But is this enough?

No, it's not enough. Because being okay with failing can feel so . . . well . . . passive.

Instead, to have fulfilling and amazing careers and lives, given how rapidly business is changing, we should become masters of reinvention, actively seeking out opportunities to push ourselves into new directions and add new skills, thereby perpetually reinventing ourselves. I'd even go so far as to say we should *seek out* career curveballs, not just build resilience to them.

Feel risky?

Historically, sticking close to our proven strengths, working at established companies, playing it "safe" in our careers has been a tried-and-true strategy. Well, that was then; this is now. We know that business is changing rapidly . . . and that if you're not changing, too, you're getting left behind. You're actually taking on *more* career risk (in my opinion) by staying put than if you actively push yourself in new directions. Failure to reinvent is a career risk many people don't even know they're taking.

You may be saying, "Well, sure that's the case in tech companies or start-ups." Or in media. Or in the manufacturing industry. But I don't work in any of those fields, so I'll be okay. Well . . . are you in marketing? Because marketing is rapidly moving from being a lot about creativity to being a lot about data analytics. Are you in finance? Well, computers are becoming better "number crunchers" than humans. In investing? Technology there, too, can do many tasks better—and certainly a great deal faster—than humans. In each of these industries—and in fact just about any other one I can think of—if you're standing still professionally, you may be moving backward.

How do you know if you're stagnating? A few clues: you were one of the last of your peers on the new social network; you still "don't get" Twitter; if there's a tech project, you look down at the conference room table when they ask for volunteers to work on it; you don't spend much time with people a decade younger than you. In fact, you don't spend any time with anyone (besides your kids, if you have them) who is two decades younger than you. Innovative new projects intimidate you and you secretly sort of like pointing out why such projects at your company have failed in the past. You can only name one or two start-ups in your industry . . . and you'd never consider working for one of them anyway.

Adopt these attitudes and you'll be left in the dust: nearly 70 percent of Ellevate Network members report that they have reinvented their careers, and another 9 percent expect to.[1]

Of course, I'm one of them. It struck me recently that I've reinvented my career several times. As I recounted earlier, I was an (unhappy) investment banker in my twenties, a research analyst and director of research in my thirties, a manager of complex businesses in my forties, and now an entrepreneur in my fifties.

True, I didn't plan my career this way, at least not exactly. But I feel very fortunate that it's worked out as it has.

So, rather than waiting for reinvention to happen *to* us (a truly risky gambit), how do we take the proverbial bull by the horns and go out there and reinvent ourselves? Well, here come our familiar themes: We learn, learn, learn. We push ourselves out of our comfort zone, we take a class in something we know nothing about, we master some new technology we don't even know how to pronounce, we request challenging assignments in the areas of the company that are doing the most interesting work. We mentor, so that we are also reverse-mentored, which can keep us in the flow of new ideas. (The light bulb on this was when I visited Arianna Huffington a few years ago and noted how she surrounded herself with young people, both in the office and in her personal life. Is it a coincidence that she has been on the front end of innovative ideas?)

And there's another tool that some women may choose, as we think about reinvention. One that can be a real luxury. And one with which I have a love-hate relationship. It's the career break, or the career sabbatical.

Ah, the career break. How good does a career break sound just about now? Pretty good, right?

Many women take one: in fact, the typical woman is out of the workforce for an average of 11 years during the course of her career.[2]

Obviously there are many different reasons to take a career break. There are the necessary career breaks, which can include caring for an ailing family member; there are those that we choose to take, such as to raise a family or to change your career. There are career breaks that can advance your career and advance your thinking, and career breaks that can set you back in your career. And I should know, since I've taken three career breaks myself.

My first career break—when I quit my tough investment

banking job—was key for me. It enabled me to get out of a world that was not my calling, to say the least, and give myself the opportunity to reflect on what I liked about it and what I didn't, how I wanted to spend my days, and what I was good and not so good at. It helped me realize that I wanted to do something that involved analytics (which I love), building Excel models (which I adore—seriously), writing (which I like . . . sort of), and engaging with smart people (which I also love). And it had a great deal of personal accountability. Oh yes, and some flexibility.

After months of going around and around on this, one day, while standing in the kitchen eating a pear, I had a lightning-bolt insight: I wanted to be an equity sell-side research analyst (as I like to say: the dream of so many young women).

It was one of the great insights of my life and set me up for the next leg of my career, which ended with my running Smith Barney. But the career break was not without its cost. First of all, I had to get back into the workforce . . . and in doing so, I was rejected by—get ready for it—Goldman Sachs, Lehman Brothers (three times), Merrill Lynch, Dillon Read, UBS, Deutsche Bank, Salomon Brothers, DLJ, Nomura, Credit Suisse, First Boston, Dain Rauscher, PaineWebber, Bankers Trust, J.P. Morgan, Alex Brown, and Smith Barney, where the word came back to me that the director of research didn't think I would work very hard. (You know what they say about karma: I later ended up firing him when he worked for me . . . but not for that reason.) Morgan Stanley was midway through offering me a job, and then rescinded it— because they had found out I was (oh dear) a new mother. I finally got a job offer from Sanford Bernstein. It was worth the wait, and as you read earlier, it was a firm at which I loved working.

That was a valuable career break. It moved my career forward in a meaningful way. I recognize that in this I was lucky. That not everyone has the luxury of voluntarily taking time out of the work force to "find themselves," especially when there are bills to pay.

I also recognize that sometimes career breaks are not voluntary. People get laid off, reorganized out, restructured out, fired, and find themselves on a very different kind of career break. These career curveballs happen, and while we may wish they didn't, we can either throw up our hands in despair or we can choose the curveballs—and use them to our advantage.

I've had a few of these "involuntary" career breaks. My first one was, in hindsight, a complete waste of time. This was after I was booted out of Citi for returning client funds (so, not my choice . . . not by a long shot). I spent it moping around waiting to get an offer from Bank of America (which, I mentioned earlier, I then negotiated poorly).

My second unwelcome break, after I left Bank of America, turned out (so far) to be my best. Instead of licking my wounds, as I'd done after getting the ax from Citi, I approached this one as an opportunity to think about what I had loved in my last set of jobs, what I didn't love anymore, what I wanted to do in my next phase, and what I wanted to continue to learn. Most of all, like so many women I know, I thought about the impact I wanted to have and what my mission for the next stage of my career would be.

What made the difference was that while I was passive about my second career break ("Here's me networking—sure hope someone calls me with a great job!"), this time I decided to take an active approach. ("This is the kind of job I want. Here's me going after the skills I need to do it and meeting the people who can help me do it.") I decided to embrace my inherent love of learning. That is, I decided to figure out what knowledge gaps I wanted to fill in and then actively set out to fill them.

I did this by spending time in Silicon Valley, where I've met some of the most kick-ass female entrepreneurs. I actively explored social media. I spent time in Washington, D.C., helping leaders on Capitol Hill understand the workings of Wall Street in the wake of the financial crisis; I looked at jobs outside of financial services. I proactively pursued board positions that were different from the traditional corporate ones I had had in the past, and I dug into mentoring some young entrepreneurs in New York. . . . As noted earlier, I'm pretty sure I learned more from them than they did from me.

And during this career break, I had the second lightning-bolt, career-changing insight of my life. This one happened while I was applying mascara, not while eating a pear. The epiphany, that the retirement savings crisis is a women's crisis, was what set me on my newest course.

It's a women's crisis because we retire with two-thirds the money that men have and live five-plus years longer. That means we're far more likely to spend the final years of our life at best just scraping by, and at worst totally broke. And if you recognize that this is a women's crisis, many potential solutions to it change: it's no longer just about tax increases or saving Social Security; it's about women earning more, staying in the workforce longer . . . and (here's the biggie for me) investing more.

I became consumed with solving the problem of what I call the "gender investing gap." Given my background in financial services and how much I care about advancing women, it seemed like the natural move.

My first thought was to take this to some big-company CEO so that he could tackle it. Boy, that didn't work. Here's one conversation. Me: "And ninety percent of women manage their money on their own at some point in their lives." Him: "But don't their husbands manage their money for them?" Me: big sigh. This really happened.

Some years ago I would have sighed at his shortsightedness, had a big glass of wine, griped about the issue to some friends, and moved on. But those passive days, for me, were over. So in 2015 I pulled together a team to start Ellevest, which we conceived as a digital investment platform for women. The typical business advice to women today (essentially, at work, "act like a man") is scarily similar to what the investments industry implicitly demands ("invest like a man"). So, as I like to tell the team, our goal is "to meet women where they are" and give them a platform for investing their money in the way that feels right to them.

What does "investing like a woman" mean, exactly? Our research tells us that women see investing not as a way to outperform markets (the target of so much of the industry today) but as a way to reach our life goals. So looking for the hot new stocks is not what we do at Ellevest. Instead we help women build a full financial plan, through which they can plan for their big goals in life. We build highly customized investment portfolios for each goal a woman wants to achieve, whether it's to start her business, or buy a home, or retire well; we've built a planning and investing algorithm that takes into account things like she will live longer than men on average, and her salary will peak sooner (both of which matter—a lot—for financial planning). And we also alert her when she's off track for her goals. (Believe it or not, zero percent of the people I've spoken to have had a feel for whether they are on or off track in regard to what they want to achieve in life financially.)

As we built this, any number of folks said, "Well, why for women? Why not build it for everyone?" Well, part of the reason a platform like this is so sorely needed by women—and indeed part of the reason women retire with two-thirds less money—is directly related to the career break we've been talking about.

Because here's the thing: career breaks can be expensive. Sure, you're probably saying, if I take a two-year career break and I make $85,000 a year, that's me out $170,000. That's a pretty expensive career break, you must be thinking.

Um, yeah, it's even worse. A lot worse. At that salary level, that career break can actually cost you more than $1 million over the course of your career.[3]

Huh, what?

According to an Ellevate Network survey, many women reported a pay cut of 20 percent or more after taking a career break. (Even worse, at the time of the survey, some 20 percent hadn't been able to find a job to come back to yet.[4]) Assume that 20 percent salary cut, and that you're then getting raises off a lower salary for the rest of your career, and—well, I won't bore you with the math, but trust me when I say those dollars add up fast.

What this means is that financially a career break may only make sense if you can use it to boost your skills, do some real soul-searching about what you want to do next, or transition to a new role.

I know how fortunate I was to be able to give myself the gift of time as I did some real soul-searching and decided to embark on this entrepreneurial phase of my career. Not everyone can take the time off, I know. But any time off you can give yourself—a weekend on your own to just sit and think, a weekly evening with friends also engaged in self-reinvention, some good therapy, anything that has you asking yourself important questions—can pay off.

So, my best advice is to allow yourself to dream a bit, as you find your way from one career stage to the next. And even if you don't have the financial safety net to take a full-fledged career break, continue to challenge yourself to keep learning and to take career risks. Once you're comfortable in your job, that might be the time to get a bit uncomfortable. So ask for the new project; join a nonprofit board that can expand your skills; take an online coding class; make the lateral move into a new department; freelance on the side to boost your skills; spend time with people who are innovating in your industry; and read, read, read. Whatever you can do to keep yourself moving forward will help you remain in a state of reinvention; it will reduce your career risk, and, honestly, it can simply make your life a lot more interesting and fun.

CHAPTER 9

The Best Career Advice No One Is Talking About

This chapter is about getting yourself in financial control and investing in your future. Now that I've said that, are you tempted to skip this chapter?

Please don't.

As you're thinking about flipping ahead, I'll bet you're also thinking, *What the heck is a chapter like this doing in a book that's so much about women and work? And power? And recognizing our worth? And accelerating positive change in the world?*

But in truth it couldn't be more related. This chapter is here because, as we all know, money is power. Financial independence is power: it's the power to make a career switch, the power to negotiate with our boss with confidence, the power to start our own business. The power to go back to school and get an advanced degree, to explore nontraditional job opportunities, to invest in ourselves in ways that will help us be more successful—and more fulfilled—in our careers. It's also the power to leave a bad marriage, the power to help an aging parent, the power to retire early—maybe even on a beach somewhere. The power to live our lives fully. I believe that only when we are truly secure in our finances can we be truly secure in our careers.

So what's the best career advice that no one is talking about? Invest your money.

I mean it. Because investing your money may end up being more important for your future than any career move you ever make. How important?

Well, remember that raise we talked about in Part I and the compounding effect it can have on your lifetime earnings? Remember how just a 2 percent higher raise each year from a starting salary of $50,000 can add up to an extra $943,000 in yearly income after thirty years? Or the additional $1.1 million we can earn over the course of forty years if we were to close our individual gender gap, and get that raise to bring our salary on par with what the guy in the office next door is making?[1]

Yes, getting that raise matters. But it drives me nuts that so many personal finance writers imply it's the *only* thing that matters: "Well, sure, women should invest more . . . but, really, until we get the gender pay gap fixed, we haven't solved the real problem, so why bother?"

Stop right there. That's a bit like saying "Hey, you broke your arm. But your leg's broken, too. Until you get your leg fixed, you haven't solved the real problem, so let's just not do anything about that arm."

This type of thinking is part of the reason that, according to data from the investment firm BlackRock, we women default to keeping some 68 percent of our savings in cash (and here I don't just mean dollar bills under our mattresses—though that's a bad idea, too—but in checking and savings accounts) instead of in diversified investment portfolios that have historically been higher yielding over time.[2]

Now, having money in cash can feel pretty good. It feels safe. But the cost of that (mostly false) sense of security is a high one. When our money is in cash, we lose ground every day, as the interest we earn on that cash fails to keep up with the corrosive impact of inflation. By standing still, we are actually moving backward.

What if we invest that money instead?

Now get ready to hold on to your hat. Because what I call the gender investing gap (the fact that women are less likely to invest their savings than men) can cost us tens of thousands, or even hundreds of thousands of dollars (for some even more)—over the course of our lives.

In fact, for some women, the "gender investing gap" may be costing us more than the "gender pay gap." Let's let that sink in: the investing gap may be costing some of us more than the gender pay gap.

The numbers: let's say you earn $85,000 a year and are regularly saving 20 percent of it in the bank (for retirement and other big goals). If instead you were to invest that money in a diversified investment portfolio (say 5 percent over time) instead of earning 1 percent in a bank, you could earn another $1.5 million to $2 million+ over the next forty years. That includes good and bad markets. Of course, that 5 percent you get from a portfolio does not come without some risk, and some years the returns will likely be negative. In other years the returns may be higher than 5 percent. But history would indicate that over the long term, a 5 percent expected return is quite reasonable.[3]

A 5 percent return may not feel like a lot more than a 1 percent return, and it's not in any given year. But now let's layer on the concept of compounding, or what Albert Einstein reportedly called "the eighth wonder of the world." The power of compounding means that if you invest $1,000 today and earn 10 percent on it in the coming year, you have $1,100. If you earn that same 10 percent return the next year, you earn it on the $1,100. So you earn $110, not $100. So after, say, ten years of earning 5 percent, that same $1,000 has grown to $1,550 (as opposed to the $1,095 if you'd kept it in the bank). And so on and so on. And after another ten years, and another ten times, it adds up to a lot.

This isn't intuitively obvious to many of us, and so it causes us to underestimate by a good amount the positive impact investing can have on our finances and our lives.

Let's hit the compounding issue from a different angle. This time, like so many other women, you are planning to invest. You really are. Definitely going to. You've got lots of investing books ready for review; they're right there, on your bedside table. But . . . then you decide tonight's not really a good time to dive in. You're tired. They just put a whole season of your favorite show on Hulu. You'd rather read that new novel you just downloaded. Whatever. Tomorrow night, same story. And the next night and next night. And before you know it a year and then a decade has gone by.

Taking my same example, you are making $85,000 a year, saving 20 percent in the bank, and not investing. Any guess as to what the cost per day of waiting that decade can be? Anyone? Anyone?

It's $100 a day. That's right: $100 a day on average.

So let me ask you something: If you had a hole in your purse, and $100 fell out of it every day, how many days would it take you to fix your purse? Probably not a decade.

But that's basically what you're doing if you don't invest.

So that's what investing can do for us as individuals. Now think about us as a group, because, remember, together we women control $5 trillion in investable assets. Let's say that much of that $5 trillion is in cash and that it's yielding 1 percent a year. What if we were to collectively invest just $1 trillion of it—just $1 trillion of our $5 trillion in assets—in a diversified investment portfolio, one that on average earns 5 percent a year?

We would earn $50 billion on those assets a year . . . or $40 billion more than if we left it in cash. That's not just serious money; that's serious power.

What's standing in our way from owning that power?

One barrier is that money is perceived to be such a tough subject: in fact, women report that money is their number one source of stress, and so we avoid dealing with it.[4]

We stress because we worry that we don't have enough money. Or we stress that we don't know what enough is. We stress because we don't have a financial plan or even know what one should look like. We stress because we think we're bad with money (spoiler alert: we're not), or because we're overwhelmed by the amount of investing advice out there, and don't even know where to start (the problem I'm working on). We stress because money is the number one thing we argue about with our spouses and partners.[5] (It is the *only* thing I remember my parents arguing about, and those fights were the hide-under-the-bed-until-it-passes kind of stuff for us kids.)

In fact, the stress is so significant that research shows it can cost us two weeks of productivity annually at work. Even more money left on the table!

With this stress comes shame. Shame because we think we should be more proactive with our money. Shame because we think we spend too much of it. Shame because we make less than our friends or siblings or partners. Shame because we make *more* than our friends or siblings or partner. Shame because we fear we're not having enough of an impact with our money. Shame because we know we should be saving for our goals in life, and we should be more actively investing it—but we're not. And yet we can also feel shame if we are actively investing, since this has traditionally implied that we're somehow less feminine.

If I were to go all Gloria Steinem on us, I would say it's in large part because of the messages we've received for so long from society, from the press, and from the industry that investing is hard for women, that investing is too complicated for our female-size brains to understand, or that investing is the "man's job" in a partnership or marriage. The shame comes from media messages that women just need "more hand-holding" around investment (ugh, seriously?), and that we need more "financial education" . . . and more and more . . . before we'll be prepared to manage our money well. The message of investing not being "for us" because of all the war and sports analogies the industry uses ("beat the market," "outperform," "pick a winner") . . . and the industry's bull. Very traditionally male stuff that we couldn't possibly relate to or understand.

We have received these messages throughout the course of our lives and they have served to keep the keys to the kingdom from us.

Okay, so if we feel stress and we feel shame about money, what do we do in response? Everything in our power to avoid thinking or talking about the subject. In fact, I'd go so far as to say that among women, talking about money is the last existing taboo in a culture where few other topics are considered too private to talk about any longer. I remember meeting with a group of women, the leaders of the Ellevate Network chapter in Philadelphia, some time ago. As we went around the table to introduce ourselves, the conversation turned to sex. One of the women mentioned that she was undergoing in vitro fertilization treatment, then there was a joke about what that meant for her sex life, and the next thing you know the group was laughing about how often they did (or did not) have sex. This conversation was happening, mind you, among a group of women who barely knew one another, and it was being conducted without a hint of embarrassment or shame.

I remember thinking how I could stop that conversation absolutely cold if I started asking the women about money . . . about how much they each had saved and invested. I could imagine the hugely awkward silence that would follow, the uncomfortable squirming and the downcast eyes. But seriously. It's twisted, but true: for women, it's somehow become more acceptable to over-share about what happens in the bedroom and the state of our ovaries than it is to talk about how we invest our money.

This is true even for the most accomplished, financially savvy women. I also remember having coffee with one absolutely kick-ass female entrepreneur, a self-made multimillionaire, someone whose name you would recognize. I was talking to her about my idea for Ellevest. To my utter surprise, she revealed to me that she had all of her (substantial) money in the bank, because she didn't trust Wall Street, because she didn't have enough time to dig in on investing, because she really hated being made to feel dumb.

Like so many women we spoke to as we were conducting our research for Ellevest, she keeps a stack of books on investing next to her bed, and she vows to get to them so that she can learn about investing ... but then she never does. So the money sits in the bank and earns nothing.

Now, that multimillionaire entrepreneur I mentioned will, of course, be okay. But for most people, there can be real conse-quences to our avoiding the topic of money.

Not convinced? Well (just in case the argument for the finan-cial upside wasn't enough for you), here's a cautionary tale about what can happen when we don't take control of our money—and instead leave our financial destiny to others (men) to decide. Because I've been there, too. Even though I grew up in a solidly middle-class family and even though I went to work on Wall Street right out of college, I've been out of financial control at times in my life. (Yes, I really do learn everything the hard way.)

I married my college sweetheart a year after graduation. We were both working in finance. I was in New York; he was in Lon-don. We couldn't stand to be apart, but our parents would have had a breakdown if we had lived together "in sin," as they put it (it was the eighties, we're Southern), so we got married. We were living the dream: two years in London, then back to New York, where we were both building our careers. I went to business school, he continued in his job.

And then there were a couple of signs of something being amiss. Not big signs, just little ones. His career trajectory started to flatten out a bit; he no longer seemed to be the golden boy at work. Management, apparently, liked him better in London than New York.

He traveled a lot. He brooded some. We bickered more, over dumb things. He left my sister's wedding weekend early "for work." When I returned, the guest room curtains were tied back incorrectly, and there was a hair on the bedspread that did not appear to be mine.

I made a note to myself to ask him if he was having an affair . . . and promptly forgot to. Finally, after Sunday night dinner (I made Spanish tortillas, salad, and apple pie), I asked. He said no. I asked again; he said no again. I wanted to believe him, but something didn't feel quite right—so I asked one more time. His response: "You're gonna be mad."

Yes. Yes, I was mad. And devastated. My vision became suddenly distorted and it looked to me as though he were a cartoon character pulled down a tube.

In the days that followed, I lost weight like it was water. I hadn't cried like that—long, long bouts of tears—since I was a child. Worse, I was just a couple of weeks away from starting my first post-business-school job; on the first day, I had to leave between orientation sessions to vomit.

In addition to the typical painful emotions around the ending of a marriage, my pain was also partly financial. While I had been the one making the Spanish tortillas, he had been the one who was paying the bills and making the financial decisions. I never, ever, ever expected my marriage to end, so the division of labor felt like it made sense. But now I felt like an idiot. Here I was, building a career on Wall Street, and I realized I didn't even know how much money we had as a couple or where we were investing it or spending it. Today I am very involved in my family's financial decisions, and I haven't been able to bring myself to make tortillas since.

Of course, that type of arrangement—the husband deals with the finances while the wife deals with, well, everything else—is far from rare, even today. Most of us know someone or indeed many people in this boat: smart, accomplished women who, though they might have advanced degrees and IQs through the roof, have no idea what's going on with their finances because, somehow, that's "their husband's job." A friend of mine recently lost her husband suddenly, and he left her not only in mourning but with a financial mess as well. He'd always assured her everything was fine, but it wasn't. When he died, it fell to her to sort everything out, and what she found was massive debt and no retirement savings. She had to sell their family home, take on a second job, and cut back drastically on her lifestyle and on her daughters'. She even had to give away one of the family dogs. This is a story I hear all the time, yet few of us imagine it can happen to us.

So it's up to us to take financial control of our lives, if only as a means of "playing defense"—as insurance just in case the unimaginable or the unexpected happens. Given how important this is, how can we overcome these fears and taboos that exist around money, and take control of our financial lives? My answer is that *just as we can take control of our career in the workplace by giving ourselves permission to play the success game our way, so, too, can we take control of our money by giving ourselves permission to approach investing our way.*

Just as we women can approach the workplace differently than men do, we can also approach investing differently. Not worse (in fact, I would argue pretty strongly in this case, better), but differently, and this is where all the female traits you read about in Part I come into play.

First, our risk awareness. Men tend to focus on the investment upside, whereas women are about protecting our downside first. Next up: long-term perspective. The (male-dominated) industry targets outperforming the market on a quarterly or yearly basis. My research shows that women are more about reaching our long-term goals, like retiring well or buying their first home. Moreover, men tend to check their investment portfolios more frequently; women less so. All of this results in an investment strategy likely to yield better results over the long term.[6]

The list goes on. Men tend to approach investing product by product; women tend to look first for a financial plan. (Remember that holistic perspective we take?) And we women invest more in companies and causes with missions and convictions we believe in, rather than chase trends or simply invest according to the gut.

See? Different. But not worse.

So, with our money, just as in the workplace, if we can give ourselves permission to embrace and even double down on our inherent female strengths, we will unleash tremendous financial power, both as individuals and collectively. We can own this.

So how do we get from here to there? Well, the first step is to acknowledge and reject the myths and even the half-myths that have built up around women and investing. And some of them are truly deeply rooted. They include:

Myth 1: Women are not "as good at math"—and mathlike things—as men. Not true. On this the research is conclusive. Females are every bit as good at math as males.[7] (Yup, and at science, too, by the way.)

Myth 2: Women need more financial education to invest. Well, I certainly won't go on record as arguing against more financial education for anyone. But this is a real red herring because *everyone* needs more financial education, but that doesn't mean it should keep us from investing. I mentioned before that when I was at Smith Barney, our research showed that neither gender understood what a managed account was, despite it being our biggest product. Neither gender would ask, but the men would invest in the product and the women wouldn't. And it left the men better off. So both genders can stand more financial education, of course. But it's holding women back more than it is with men.

The truth is that investing isn't as complex or as risky or as difficult as people think. I'm not saying it's not a little scary to entrust the markets with our hard-earned money, particularly when those markets are volatile, but the act of investing itself is really not all that complicated. And we *don't* need to know everything to get started. So more education, yes. But waiting until we feel like we know everything there is to know about investing? Not necessary.

Myth 3: Men are better investors than women. Nope. Not the case. Women are as good investors as men, if not better.[8] This is true at the professional level—hedge fund and mutual fund managers—and at the individual level. As you read earlier, this is where our long-term orientation, our risk awareness, and our ability to see things holistically can really shine. We tend to set our investments and then let them do their thing, rather than overtrade them, and this pays off for us.

Myth 4: Women are too risk-averse to invest. Well, it's true that women are more risk-*aware*. And there is also research that says that women greatly value downside protection.[9] But this isn't a negative; in investing, this risk awareness is a virtue. It keeps many of us from making the mistakes that are so common in investing (and especially among men): chasing the hot stock, or the hot mutual fund, or the hot sector, or investing too much money in a single stock or idea, taking *more* risks and then doubling down on them when they don't seem to be paying off.[10] The research on this is clear. Our slower and steadier approach wins the race.

Myth 5: Women need more hand-holding to invest. There is a misconception that since "women are not good investors" and "don't have enough financial education," they need to hire an (expensive) financial advisor to help them with their investments. While this can be helpful for some, it's not a hurdle for all of us. In fact, we found at Ellevest that any number of women prefer a (much cheaper) online investing experience, particularly when you remove so much of the confusing jargon in investing; many referred to it as a "no-shame zone," in which they could explore their financial outlook and their financial plan in privacy.

Myth 6: Women just aren't that interested in investing. Sort of feels like they are saying we shouldn't worry our pretty little heads about these manly endeavors, doesn't it? The reality is not that women are inherently any less interested in investing, but rather that the investing industry—Wall Street—isn't well set up to serve women. There are some great, great financial advisors out there; I've worked with more of them than anyone. And there are some who do an amazing job with women; again, I've worked with more of them than anyone. But facts are facts, and the majority of women say that the investing industry doesn't serve them well. A big national study by the Boston Consulting Group found that of all the industries affecting our daily lives, women ranked financial services dead last when it came to meeting their needs.[11]

In my experience, the investing industry fundamentally frames the puzzle of women and investing incorrectly. I've spoken to many CEOs on this topic, all of whom ask the question "How can we better *market* to women?" In other words, they assume that their offerings are the right ones for women and that their means of engaging with women is the right one, too—it's just their *marketing* that's the problem. I don't believe this to be the case.

I'll give you an example. When I was CEO of Merrill Lynch, we spent hundreds of millions of dollars a year on our investment organization—the vast majority of the money focused on picking investments that would go up (that is, higher risk, higher return). As for our investment in asset *protection*—that is, avoiding losses—to say it was an afterthought is being kind to afterthoughts. So our offering was very geared to what men were looking for—risk.

We could have—and did—try all sorts of different means of marketing our existing products to women. But we missed the fundamental point. We weren't marketing to women incorrectly; we were *serving* women incorrectly. It is as though today's investing industry is speaking Chinese, and women are speaking French.

It's a totally different language and a different approach. To me, it's probably not a coincidence that an industry where more than 85 percent of its financial advisors are men—and whose management teams that went into the downturn were white, male, and middle-aged, and came out whiter, maler, and "middle-aged-er"—hasn't met the challenge of serving female customers.

Okay, so you're over the myths. You're ready to take financial control.

The first step? As in so much of life, avoiding common mistakes is half the battle. In my experience, these are the top eight financial mistakes women make.

1. Letting your husband or partner manage the money without your involvement.

Very 1964 . . . and not in the cool, mod Beatles concert way. Few of us think we'll get divorced or that tragedy will strike, but it does. As I learned the hard way, you don't want to be introducing yourself to your financial situation while you're in emotional shock.

2. Signing your joint income tax return without reading it. This is the mistake that divorce specialists often cite. If your husband hands those tax returns to you at the last minute with a "Don't worry, just sign it, honey," please don't do it without reading it. You're on the hook if there's a mistake in there.

3. Using your husband's or partner's financial provider, even if you don't know or can't stand him. (And he is usually a "him.") Here's a test: at your next joint meeting, how much does the advisor engage you/speak to you/look at you? If he spends most of his time talking to your husband, find your own money person or firm. This is one of those situations where trusting our instincts is essential.

4. Not asking for jargon to be explained. Don't let politeness—or shyness, or embarrassment, or anything else—get in the way of getting the information you need to understand your finances. And keep asking until you understand. It's your money, and your right. If you are working with an advisor who won't give you an explanation that you understand, it's not you, it's him or her. Move on.

5. Not taking into account your greater longevity in your investing plan. If you're married, remember that you're likely to live five-plus years longer than he does. Does your financial plan take this into account, and your years without him? Even if both of you are "moderate risk" investors, that means different things if you're living longer.

6. Not buying long-term care insurance. Here's a shocker: 70 percent of sixty-five-year-olds will need some form of long-term care.[12] And, again, we're around for five-plus years longer than he is.

7. Not taking enough smart investing risks. I've noted that we women tend to be more risk-aware in our investing. While this may sound counterintuitive, our longer lives—and the fact that we retire with two-thirds the retirement savings of men—can call for somewhat greater (but still prudent) risk-taking, for the potential to earn a higher return. If the market goes down, our greater longevity may actually give us more time to recover.

8. Waiting until a less risky time to invest . . . or procrastinating. "Gee, the market feels iffy." Or "I feel like I need to get through that stack of reading on the markets." Or "I'll find time later. Really, I will." If you want to, you can find many reasons to wait to invest. But timing the markets is almost impossible, even for people who do it full-time. Investing steadily over time may help to smooth out the market ups and downs . . . and is historically a vastly better alternative than keeping your money in cash. Besides which, investing shouldn't be a one-time, "you're right or wrong" thing; instead you should invest steadily. That means sometimes you'll "buy low" and sometimes you'll "buy high"; it may even out.

So those are the don'ts. Now what about the dos? Don't worry, I'm not going to recycle the watered-down finance advice we've all heard a million times, like "Give up you morning latte and invest that money instead" (relayed in a perky, upbeat manner). Sheesh . . . come on, guys.

Instead these are the basics.

1. Pay off your high-interest debt, such as credit card debt. That stuff is poison. You buy a $1,000 piece of electronic equipment on credit, at a 20 percent rate of interest (which is not unusual), and if you pay the minimum balance it will take you four years to pay it off, tacking on $471 in interest. That's bad enough. But, remember, you are paying that bill off out of your after-tax income. And if that money had been invested you'd be making money off it that whole time. So do yourself a favor and pay it off, as fast as you can.

2. Make sure you have an emergency fund in place. This should be at least three months' worth of salary (six is even better) . . . because stuff can happen. And stuff is expensive.

(By the way: Worst financial advice ever is to build up your emergency fund before you pay off your credit card debt. Worst.

Financial. Advice. Ever. I can't believe how many self-styled finance experts—and particularly those who claim to give advice specifically for women—recommend building an emergency fund before you fully pay off your credit card debt. That means it'll cost you *a lot of* money to borrow money on your credit card ... and then essentially have that money sitting in a bank account earning nothing. Huh? Much better to pay off the credit card now, have no money in the bank, and then borrow on the credit card later if there's an emergency and you must.)

3. Once the emergency fund is built, save. Save as much as you can. The guideline that has been shown to work best is to save 20 percent of your salary. Yes, I know you've heard this one before, and I know 20 percent can feel like a lot, particularly in a country in which the savings rate is closer to 0 percent. But research from consumer rights advocate Senator Elizabeth Warren and others shows that people who put aside this much do better through economic ups and downs. This means splitting your paycheck up this way: 50 percent for needs, 30 percent for wants, and 20 percent for savings and paying down debt.

Whatever you decide you can manage to save, be sure to put that amount aside first, rather than waiting to see what's left over after your spending (as some people say, "Pay yourself first"). If you spend first and save what's leftover, I'm betting it won't be enough. A good place to start is to max out your 401(k) contributions at work.

4. Invest. You've already read about how much more money you stand to make over a lifetime if you invest your savings rather than leave them in cash. Just do it. Find a financial relationship you are comfortable with, either a person or a digital advisor like Ellevest, or more traditional online providers like Vanguard or Charles Schwab. Invest in index funds or low-cost ETFs that in turn invest in broad markets such as the S&P 500 or the MSCI World.

5. Target saving 11 to 15 times your salary for retirement. I know this seems like a lot—and it is—but think about it: you may be retired for twenty, thirty, or more years. And you need to support yourself—hopefully comfortably—during those years; you make $80,000 a year and want to live on that in retirement, you will need close to $1 million if you retire at sixty-five and live to your life expectancy.

6. Buy insurance. Having life insurance will put your family in better shape if either you or your partner passes away. This is especially important if you have dependent children. Long-term care insurance can also pay off hugely if you or your partner becomes disabled and can't work.

7. Put together a will. I don't care if you're twenty years old or seventy. If you want your assets to go where you want them to go once you're gone (instead of, you know, just to the government), then you need a will.

8. Don't just hope for–*plan for*–the things you want in life. No matter what your financial goals are—whether it's to buy a second home, pay for your kid's college, or retire in style—you need a financial plan. For example, want to start a business? At Ellevest, we recommend saving twenty-four months of your salary, to give yourself the runway to give the business a shot of working. Want to have a baby? Boy, they're expensive. Up that emergency fund to nine months . . . because all sorts of things come up when you have a child. Want to buy a home? Check home prices in your area with Zillow; you'll want to save 20 percent of the cost for a down payment. How about a career break? Remember, they're more expensive than you think they are—by a lot. So if that's in the cards for you, save enough to replace your salary dollar for dollar for the time you plan to spend out of the workforce.

For each of these life goals, planning ahead is the difference between actually achieving them and just dreaming about them.

A note on your financial plan. Many people think of this as

a "big thing": pages and pages of numbers. And it can be. But it's better to get started and have something, even if it's a one-page document, than to wait until you have a detailed twenty-page plan in place. The first step can be to track inflows and outflows: what you earn, what you spend, and what you save. And your first goal is to make sure they're in balance. Then start to lay out what you want to achieve in life, and the big things you're saving for, and make sure you're tracking toward achieving those, by saving enough toward them. And then iterate, adjust, and update this over time. It doesn't have to be perfect right away to be a useful guide.

Look, I get that doing this stuff isn't at the top of any list of how we want to spend our time. Neither is exercising for me. But I do it to stay healthy. So try to look at all this like the treadmill for your finances. Spending just twenty minutes a day on it isn't so bad and will go a long way in improving your long-term financial fitness.

Besides, being in financial control is in itself healthy: one study showed that employees who contributed to a 401(k) plan had improved blood test results and health behaviors *27 percent more often* than those who did not contribute to a retirement plan; this was possibly the result of lower stress. And a survey by TD Bank reported that simply having a financial plan in place made 80 percent of respondents feel satisfied with their overall health and well-being.

I get that it can be no fun. A friend of mine says that it's like flossing for her. For some, it's more like getting a cavity filled. But think about it this way: would you get a cavity filled for those tens of thousands or hundreds of thousands or millions of dollars this may be costing you that we talked about earlier? Yeah, me, too.

And isn't it even more worth it so that we can demonstrate its importance to our daughters? Our actions can be even more powerful than our words.

And the power that comes from our owning our financial futures? It's the best career move no one else is talking about. Think about it this way. You're already working hard to make more money at work, so why not work just a little bit harder to make that money work hard for you?

PART III

The Courageous Conversations

Okay, by now we know that, as women, we have a lot of things going for us. In business we are great assets and leaders with plenty to offer. Having us around and in power in greater numbers improves corporate culture, company performance, the economy, and society. And the world is going more our way, as the qualities we bring to the workforce become even more valuable.

But ... you know ... that doesn't mean we can necessarily count those in power (that is, the guys) to hand us leadership positions, treat us well, or pay us what we're worth just because it's the right or the smart thing to do. Or even because the research shows that it's in their own best interest. Let's face it, this has been an issue for years and years.

I've probably worked with as many men in senior positions in business as anyone else out there. I've probably walked into as many conference rooms and interrupted as many guys deep in conversation as anyone else out there. And you know what I've never heard? "Hey, Sallie. Funny you should walk in now. We were just discussing the importance of gender diversity in driving corporate performance."

Never.

Not once.

So if we want these conversations to be had—and we do—to a good degree, it's up to us to start them, to bring up these topics, to raise these issues. And to bring the guys into them. To help them along. If we don't, the guys *may* eventually get it, and things *may* eventually change. Eventually. But I don't want to sit around and wait for the guys to get with the program, do you?

If we want change on our timelines and on our terms, we need to have what Ellyn Shook, the chief human resources officer of Accenture, recently called the "courageous conversations" around gender inequality and sexism in the workplace.

Sheryl Sandberg initiated a "courageous conversation" with the publication of *Lean In*. (And the initial backlash demonstrated just how courageous she was being.) Anne-Marie Slaughter initiated a "courageous conversation"—and, for a time, something of a firestorm—with her article in *The Atlantic* that basically said women could not "have it all."[1] And Judith Williams certainly initiated a "courageous conversation" at the 2015 SXSW conference when she called out Eric Schmidt for repeatedly interrupting the Chief Technology Officer of the United States government, Megan Smith, on the subject of gender inequities in tech, of all things. (Oh, and Williams was running Google's Global Diversity and Talent Program, which made Schmidt the chairman of her company, and her boss.) Now those are some courageous conversations.

Luckily you don't have to write a book, or take the stage at SXSW, or be a CEO to initiate our own courageous conversation. We all have the power to bring about change, individually and collectively, and the way we do that is by each of us starting conversations in our own workplaces.

Courageous conversations don't have to be just about the big stuff, either; they don't have to address the systemic roots of sexism in society or tackle closing the gender pay gap. You can initiate a courageous conversation about seemingly minor gender inequity in the workplace, such as calling attention to a woman not being offered a big assignment on the assumption she won't want it because she's pregnant. (You'd better believe I saw this happen.) Or pointing out that a woman was dinged for being "aggressive" in her performance review while a man was celebrated for it.[2] (I saw this, too.) Or calling out a male co-worker for condescending to or "man-terrupting" a female peer.

And initiating these conversations *can* work, like the time I saw a lone board member ask to see the company's pay rate by gender, and then convince the board to give the women raises to get rid of the gap. (It was beautiful.)

Why do I think these courageous conversations can work? In addition to seeing it in action, research shows that they get results on a broader scale. As just one example, research done by She Should Run exploring the effect of sexist coverage of political candidates has shown that when sexist comments are made about female candidates—either nasty ones, like "She's an airhead," or even seemingly complimentary ones, like "She's got great legs"— the female candidate suffers in the polls. If, however, that female candidate *calls out* those comments as being sexist, her poll results improve.[3]

So, while I may have considered these "courageous conversations" to be risky in the past (risky that I'd upset someone, or goodness forbid, come off as hysterical, or a raging feminist)—I now believe that it is riskier *not* to have them.

That's because if we're *not* having these conversations, those old gender expectations and beliefs that have in part kept us from moving forward professionally will continue on, unchallenged.

We have to pick our battles, of course. And timing can be everything. This is not a conversation one necessarily wants to have on the first day in a new job, for example. We are more likely to be effective once we have built up some "political capital." But in general, having more courageous conversations over the course of the day-to-day in the workplace will keep the issue on the front burner and can educate those around us. Ultimately, awareness and education are what lead to progress.

In this section, I want to walk through a handful of the "courageous conversations" we can be having, ones that can pay off for us quickly. They can help us on a personal level by making it clear we are serious and paying attention. And they can pay off over the long term by paving the way for real cultural change.

I also firmly believe that owning these conversations can also position each of us as true leaders, for taking a principled and educated stance on what is clearly "the right side of history."

So let's talk about what these conversations within our organizations can be, and how to have them.

CHAPTER 10

Let's Hold a Funeral for the Diversity Council . . . and Other Well-Meaning Initiatives That No Longer Work

When it comes to conversations on values that matter, diversity can be a big one. Diversity matters in making companies the types of places at which we want to work—the kinds of places where employees are engaged, innovation flourishes, and everyone is given the freedom to embrace their individuality and thrive. And it matters for shaping companies to have a positive impact on the world around them—the meaning and purpose we've talked so much about.

So, how do you read between the lines of a company's core values before you decide to work there? Specifically, how do you know if part of that culture is valuing diversity? And our uniqueness as individuals and as women?

Well, we may really need to dig beneath the surface on this one. At a top level, things usually seem fine: according to a recent McKinsey/LeanIn report,[1] 74 percent of companies report that their CEO is highly committed to gender diversity. But there's greater nuance than that: the same report says that fewer than half of workers actually believe it's a top priority for their immediate manager. Clearly something is getting lost somewhere along the line.

Now, there are very few companies today whose CEOs would *say* that they simply don't care about diversity. That it's not a priority for them. That it's not the right thing to do. And yet progress on diversity remains slower than most of us would like, and slower than many of us might have expected at this stage of the game.

That's not because companies don't value diversity, even if only in theory. It's simply because some of them have been approaching it in some outdated ways. So in this chapter, before we drill down on the courageous conversations we can have at work to jump-start progress, company by company by company, let's spend a little time talking about how to initiate conversations around the things that aren't working.

Lots of companies have had their diversity initiatives in place for years, if not decades. And they haven't made progress. So how about we call a halt to all of the diversity efforts that, while often well-meaning, have simply outlived their usefulness? How about we hold a funeral for the old ways of doing things and try some new ones?

I can't tell you how many years it feels like I have lost sitting in mandatory company meetings about how to advance diversity. You know, a bunch of women and people of color, as many as the HR department could scrounge up, may be sitting at a conference room table right now, making very good points and drafting very good initiatives and getting ... nothing ... at all ... done. Because, guess what? If a company's senior leadership team isn't truly committed to diversity—not just saying the words that they are, but willing to do the hard work around it—the second you leave the conference room and those proposals hit some senior person's desk, they start gathering dust.

My pet peeve: We draft these folks to work on these initiatives; we pull them away from their desks and from their real work to sit in all-day diversity council meetings or listen to speakers tell them how important diversity is. And in my old industry, and in many others like it, we don't compensate them for their lost commissions for that day; we don't extend their project deadline by a day; we don't postpone the important meeting they missed while they were gone. The result is that they were actually being penalized for dealing with the issue. No wonder, then, that at some companies people avoid those meetings like the plague. And it's pretty hard to advance the conversation on diversity if there's no one sitting around the table.

Worse, any number of companies tend to sort of cordon off the diversity initiatives as something run by people of "difference"—that is to say, the people of color, and the women—when, of course, this is not typically the group that needs convincing. It can be the ones not in the meeting who do. This can also have the effect of making it seem like this is *their* problem and so *they* need to solve it. (In my businesses, I always made sure that I had someone in the majority—and viewed as an up-and-comer at that—co-running the diversity councils, so that it was seen as everyone's issue and challenge, not just theirs.)

Another thing we spend time on that may no longer work: the "diverse slate,"* otherwise known as a mandated number of minority candidates required to be considered for each open position. A diverse slate or hiring quota that actually leads to diverse individuals getting the job on offer? Terrific. But many of us who have been in senior roles are familiar with a too-frequent outcome of the diverse slate: what's called a "slate sitter." That's the same one or two African American or Latino or female candidates who show up year after year on the list of candidates for the next-level-up job. And everyone says, "Fantastic, we have a diverse slate!" But Amy doesn't get the job because "she doesn't have marketing

---

* A slate is a list of people who are being considered for a job.

experience," or Jose doesn't get the job because "he hasn't spent time abroad." And so Amy and Jose walk away discouraged and demoralized, and on a cultural level, nothing changes.

It's worth noting that those who reflect the majority (in most cases, Caucasian men) tend to be promoted based on potential, while women tend to be promoted based on experience.[2] Without recognizing this imbalance, and taking action to put an end to it, diverse slates in and of themselves do not work.

Another thing that doesn't work?

Spending time looking for "the best person for the job."

Huh? What's wrong with looking for the best person for the job? Isn't that as American as Mom and apple pie?

In theory, looking for the "best person for the job" is perfectly fine. The issue is that when we frame it that way, our cognitive biases can kick in—fast. And when they do, that "best person for the job" can often end up being the person who looks and acts awfully similarly to us. (Occasionally I come across a picture of a leadership team where almost everyone is a white guy with male-pattern baldness. Coincidence? Doubtful.)

Why do we default to thinking that the best person for the job is, in effect, a clone of ourselves? I think it's because we can imagine, in a fully formed and vivid fashion, exactly how *we* would do the job, and of course it seems to us that that's the best way to do it. And we imagine our "clone" would do it that way.

Consciously or not (and most often it's not) we can be more comfortable working with—and promoting and advocating for—people who are just like us.

This in turn can lead to a cycle of "cascading bias," whereby the qualities valued in leadership are those of the existing leadership team. If the existing leadership is "commanding" and "decisive," and the members of the leadership team before that were "commanding" and "decisive," well, isn't it just natural that you would think that "commanding" and "decisive" are prerequisites for the role? Thus, when the same sorts of people are in the same positions year after year, it can appear to confirm biased perceptions that certain other types of persons, who bring different characteristics to the job, are less qualified to lead.[3]

The other problem with the "best person for the job" approach is that the "best" individual contributor might not be the best choice to balance out the skill sets and experience of the team. (Recall the example about a basketball team full of point guards. And the lesson that the power of diversity is . . . diversity.)

Instead of "Who is the best person for the job?" the better question is "How do I put the right team in place?" If you have a bunch of optimists on the team, it could be time to add a realist; if you have a bunch of folks who've worked at the company for a while, then it's time to add a newbie; if most of the folks are analytical, it's time for a creative . . . and if it's mostly men, how about a woman? How about other diverse individuals? That framing can help managers look for people with various and diverse strengths, and not just people who remind them of themselves.

What also doesn't work: the token woman. Or the token person of color. Or the token diverse individual of any type. One lone figure is not true diversity. And research shows that being that token person can come with a huge amount of stress and social isolation, as well as pressure to act like the majority.[4]

Exhibit A in this argument: Wall Street. I can't tell you how many women I knew on Wall Street who would take pride in assuming even more risk than the guys did, or landing bigger deals than the guys did, or executing bigger block trades than the guys did, or negotiating harder than the guys did. I completely understand why: as the only one, or the only one of a few, this could feel like (and may have been for some) the only way to get ahead. Yet in reality, as we've seen, women bring so much more to the table when they stop trying to conform to the man's version of what success looks like and instead act like their true selves at work.

151

To create a space in which we can do that, we need more than just a couple of token women in the room. I've been on a board of directors on which I was one of two women. And the two of us almost avoided spending too much time together during breaks in the board meeting, and we almost avoided chiming in to support each other on any particular issue. We never discussed it at the time; we just did it. And it's only in the past year (both of us no longer being on the board) that we've gotten together and looked back on this implicit, unspoken agreement. Both of us noted that we intuitively felt like the guys would somehow dismiss our ideas if it appeared it was the two of us "versus" them. They might think we had decided to "gang up" in some way, and therefore they would take our points of view less seriously. It sounds sort of dumb, even as I articulate these words, but that sense was there. It's also what the research indicates can frequently happen. It's very common, and very real.

My final thought on what isn't working?

I may get a lot of flack for this, but, in my opinion, the intense focus on getting women on boards of directors won't take us as far as some of its proponents think. Yes, it's great to get women onto boards—who could say no to that? But in my experience, it's not enough. Boards help the CEO set strategy. Boards act as a sounding board for the CEO. Boards represent the stakeholders and provide oversight for a company. Boards can act as a CEO's conscience and taskmaster.

But boards do *not* make the thousands and thousands and thousands of micro-decisions that set the tone at a company, that make it a great (or awful) place at which to work. That's done instead by the senior and middle management teams. Boards do not decide who is promoted to vice president of procurement or whether Susie gets the same $5,000 bonus that Joe got.

The focus on making boards more diverse is important; focusing on making middle and senior management more diverse is, in my experience, even more so. (And the good news is that it's not either/or for these two.)

It's for all these reasons that those "courageous conversations" around diversity matter so much, both about what is working, as well as what no longer works. I would argue that we should "zero-base budget" any and all diversity initiatives.* In other words, tear them up and start from scratch.

You don't have to be an executive or manager to have a say in this. You know those company-wide diversity surveys that land in your email inbox and you always mean to fill them out, but you never do? Don't do that. Take the survey. Voice your opinion. Suggest holding a funeral for the outdated initiatives at your company and building new ones instead. Suggest *not* renewing the diversity committee that is no longer driving progress and explore how diverting the resources to another diversity initiative might result in a higher return on money and time.

We shouldn't let "we've always done it" get in the way of real progress. If you believe this, initiate a courageous conversation about it.

---

* By this, I mean not automatically continue to do something just because we always did it.

CHAPTER 11

The Company Culture Conversation

How important is corporate culture? It's so important that in a recent survey, 66 percent of new business owners said they started their own business in order to build something of their own and create the kind of company they want to work for.[1] Job seekers rank corporate culture high among the top things they look for in taking a job.[2] It's so important that popular career sites like Glass-Door and The Muse include information about company culture, and others, like InHerSight, are springing up those "crowdsource" opinions on culture.

The great news about culture, particularly for us women, is that by drawing on our inherent strengths as communicators and relationship builders, we *all* have the power to help change company culture for the better—even if we're not an executive or member of the board or even in an official leadership position. And in doing so we can help advance our workplaces toward reflecting our values . . . in other words, to become places where we want to—indeed, are proud to—work.

This is even more important given that getting the culture thing right isn't just critical when it comes to our own personal satisfaction with our jobs; it's also a key factor in our companies' and our teams' performance. What if I told you that Google recently shared that the number one determinant of its teams' success is psychological safety?[3] This includes, for example, the extent to which a group's members are free to take risks without fear that they'll be humiliated, as well as how much they can trust one another. This gets down to culture. In other words, when you have a culture where people feel comfortable bringing their real selves to work, they can be more successful—more productive, more collaborative, more innovative—than those cowed by a culture of conformity or, worse, intimidation.

Do you feel safe in your workplace? Ask yourself: Can I act like myself on my team? Do I feel comfortable taking a risk? Do I know what is expected of me? Do I trust that others on my team will deliver what they say they will? If the answer to any of these questions is no, it may be time to initiate a courageous conversation about company culture.

"We must be able to talk about what is messy or sad," writes productivity and habit expert Charles Duhigg,[4] "to have hard conversations with colleagues who are driving us crazy. We can't be focused just on efficiency. Rather, when we start the morning by collaborating with a team of engineers and then send emails to our marketing colleagues and then jump on a conference call, we want to know that those people really hear us. We want to know that work is more than just labor."

To this I would add that most of us—and this is particularly true for Millennials—not only want to work in an environment that's psychologically safe; we want to work in a culture that reflects our values. Values are roadmaps to what companies stand for, what they expect of their people, and the impact they want to have in the world around them. Culture is the way a company holds itself in reflecting those values and standards.

But ... let's admit it, for some of us, corporate culture is a squishy concept. We can't really put our finger on it, and so we tend to think, *Well, if I can't even really define it, what can I really do about it anyway?*

It's a fair question. Getting a handle on company culture can be hard. The corporate value statements all sound pretty much the same, don't they? While the individual words can vary, they all tend to run along the lines of: "We place our customers at the center of everything we do." "We demand excellence of ourselves." "We value our people." Or "We take smart risks."

I've never seen "We sort of half-ass it around here most of the time." "We're too nervous about failing to take any real risks." Or "Our employees are cogs in the machine. We only value them until we don't need them any longer."

Sometimes corporate value statements truly represent what a company stands for. And sometimes they couldn't have less in common with a company's real values and culture.

Consider the following story from two companies that I know well. (Okay, really well.)

It begins with me in a cab, headed up from a meeting in downtown New York City to a lunch commitment at the Plaza hotel. When I got on the West Side Highway, my cellphone rang. It was my assistant.

"Sallie," she said, "I have one of our financial advisors on the phone for you. It's a Mr. Blow. A Mr. Joe Blow.* He says he needs to speak to you urgently." I didn't recognize his name; we had thousands of advisors.

"Okay, Allison," I said. "Please put him through."

The reason he was calling, this gentleman relayed, was that his fiancé was very sick and in the hospital. The doctors were struggling to find out what was wrong with her. He had lost confidence in them. I'll never forget his words: "Sallie, I'm scared she's going to die. I don't know who else to call."

---

* Obviously, I have changed his name.

"Okay," I told him. "Let me see what I can do."

I hung up the phone and placed a call to my CEO's office. As luck would have it, he was in Asia, where it was late at night. I relayed the advisor's story to the CEO's assistant, which she promised to relay in turn to the CEO.

I'm still on the West Side Highway, still heading to the Plaza hotel.

Okay, I remember thinking. *Now what do I do?* I began mentally going through who I knew who was on the board of what hospital. My old boss had been on a hospital board for a short time. Could he help? Or did my husband know anyone?

At this point (I'm still driving up the West Side Highway) my phone rang. It was the CEO's assistant.

"I just reached the CEO," she told me. "We've made some calls. We have doctors standing by at New York Hospital waiting for the financial advisor's fiancé. We just need to get in touch with Joe Blow to get her information and arrange for her transfer."

All this, and I'm still on the West Side Highway. It happened that quickly.

Tragically, the woman died.

But here's the point: the CEO had stopped everything he was doing, late at night, to make phone calls from halfway across the world and make something happen—to do what he could to help someone who was important to someone who worked for him. This was a CEO who was building the kind of culture in which people mattered. Really mattered. And it showed. And it wasn't just the senior people who mattered, but the fiancé of an advisor whose name he didn't even recognize.

It was clear that this was a company that valued its people. This was a company that lived its values. And I have to tell you, if you were to have listened to the conversations around the water-coolers in the days that followed, it was clear that everyone who worked for that company knew it. Which is probably why executive search people would tell me that it was very difficult to hire anyone away from that company. It had too strong a culture.

Contrast this to the second story, which takes place at a company that on paper was similar to the first. Similar lines of business. Similar set of written "core values." But there was a big difference.

This story starts as the company was reorganizing its senior leadership team, bringing in some "new blood" and thus shuffling the existing management team. On the losing end was a senior executive who had been at the company for a number of years. There weren't many who would describe this gentleman as an "A player," but he was a solid contributor and had stayed with the company through some ups and downs. He always played by the rules.

He was slated to be reorganized out that day. Unfortunately, on that particular day, he was on vacation with his family. So clearly, they would wait until he got back to fire him, right?

Wrong.

Instead his boss tracked him down on that vacation with his family ... and fired him, then and there, on the phone, in front of his wife and kids. Then, as if that humiliation weren't enough, they gave him a prepared script to read to his already assembled leadership team. That's right: after being fired, he had to tell his now-former colleagues why this reorganization and his firing were a good thing ... again, on vacation, again, in front of his family ... including his daughter ... who, by the way, had cancer.

That story, too, made the rounds at that company. It, too, was talked about at watercoolers, and in the lunchroom (this was before the days of Twitter being widespread; had it happened today, the fallout would certainly have spread much wider). It shouldn't have been surprising, really, as this incident was only one of a string of other senior firings of a similar ilk: a senior executive whose termination was announced on the day of her kid's high school graduation, another who was not allowed to return to his office but was instead escorted out the door like a criminal.

Sadly, this company isn't some rare exception; this kind of thing happens in any number of businesses. A friend of mine's husband had worked at one financial services company for thirty-five years (thirty-five years!) and was still escorted out of his office by armed guards when he was laid off. At yet another, a senior executive was given only twenty minutes' notice before the press release announcing her departure was sent out. (Oh, right, that was me.)

These kinds of business practices aren't just cruel; they're also not very smart. It's not tough to hire good people away from companies that treat their employees poorly, as you might imagine. And it's also not a stretch to understand why you don't see them on the "Best Companies" lists or among the top performers for their industries. Or winning any customer service awards. If you see your colleague treated badly or you're worried you may be next, how engaged are you going to be in your job, and how well are you going to treat your customers? Long story short: Caring about people isn't just the "right thing to do." It translates into smart business.

But in the absence of stories like these, how do you cut through the corporate boilerplate and figure out what it is that companies truly value? My advice is to work hard to assess a company's culture before you join it. Assess its actions, not just its words. Look at what its CEO is saying—and not saying. And look at the values the company is living—and not living.

Here are a few tips.

1. Get Up to Speed on the Company Lore

Of course, all the official press about a company will be pretty much sunshine and roses; not surprisingly, stories of humiliating public firings like the one I told you don't make it into the company brochure. So try to get the inside scoop, the stories that the employees tell one another in the lunchroom, at the bar, on the golf course, and so on.

When I worked at Sanford Bernstein, we would talk over a glass of wine about the contrarian stock calls our company had made over the years. We talked about all the times the *Wall Street Journal* had written about those horrible calls . . . and the times it lambasted those calls just before they worked out spectacularly well. Those moments of struggle on behalf of our clients, and then glory, were the foundation of our culture and who we wanted to be. When we talked about the types of people we hired, we always came back to the guy whose job immediately before joining Bernstein was driving a taxi. In that culture, he was a hero.

What did these stories convey? That we valued individuality and we celebrated contrarians. That struggle was a prerequisite for success.

Meanwhile, when I asked employees of the company that later bought Bernstein what stories they liked to tell, the one I heard most often was about how the CEO got drunk, threw his beer glass into a fireplace, and almost hit his business partner's wife in the head. Oh yeah, and how this incident was followed by uproarious laughter. Seriously. I'm not making this up.

The point is, there is no better place to get the inside scoop on company culture than from the stories of people who actually work there. Or, better yet, the people who used to work there.

2. Find Out How a Company Treats Exiting and Former Employees

Time and time again, the issue of culture can come back to how we treat people. If you employ and manage people in a high-performance culture, there is one near certainty: some of them will quit or be fired. But *how* a company fires can speak volumes, as we saw earlier.

If you can ask someone only one question to get to the heart of a company's underlying culture, I might suggest asking them about an employee who has left the company. Is he "that guy we were about to fire anyway" or was he "a great professional we hated to lose"? How people talk about their former employees can get to the issue of how much a place respects people as individuals.

Even better: ask a former employee himself or herself directly about a company's culture. Unlike current employees, who may be "drinking the Kool-Aid" or understand it's not in their interest to say anything negative, former employees may be far more likely to answer objectively and honestly.

Another way to get to these core issues: How does a company treat that employee *after* they fire him or her? Do they support people in finding their next job? Do they provide small courtesies, like maintaining their email address for a bit? Do they provide any career counseling? Do they maintain a strong alumni network of former employees that can provide support to the newly laid-off?

Or do they truncate any support for people the moment they walk out that door? Do they give them the bums rush to sign a separation agreement?

For those who say that cultivating a strong alumni network is not doable, or not doable at scale, Exhibit A is McKinsey, the global consulting firm. That firm is by its nature an "up-or-out" environment (i.e., over a certain period of time, you are either promoted or you are out). And yet I can't tell you how proud many of its former consultants are to have the McKinsey name on their résumé . . . or how many times I've heard them recommend fellow McKinsey alums for a job or project. Known for having one of the strangest company cultures around, McKinsey must be doing something right, and part of that something is that they support their people in finding their next job when they don't receive the next-level promotion.

Implicitly, perhaps, McKinsey recognized the positive, reinforcing power of a strong network long before many others did. Thus they cultivate that "alumni network" by keeping in touch with their former employees and bringing them back together for events and education. This respect generates immeasurable amounts of goodwill, which in turn translates to significant business sent to McKinsey by its "alums." While the financial returns on culture can be tough to quantify, this is one area in which they are most certainly positive.

So rather than working for a company with a "Don't let the door hit you in the ass on the way out" attitude, wouldn't you rather work for an employer that treats its former employees like human beings? After all, companies have plenty of employees; these people have only one career. Why *not* help them find their next opportunity if the fit is not right? Why *not* keep former employees posted with company updates, ask their opinion on issues, invite them back for cocktails, celebrate their successes, and where appropriate (think people on a career break) offer them part-time or overflow work? It costs so little and can pay off so well for the company, and for its former employees as well.

3. Look at How a Company Invests in Its Employees

Okay, the company you're looking at "values its people." But it's worth making sure it puts its money where its mouth is; that is, it's worth investigating whether it invests in making its people better.

Smart companies do, and more will increasingly recognize

this and begin asking themselves not just how this employee will perform on this or that project, but also how the company can give her or him a rich professional experience that will translate into better performance over the long term. This investment can include skills building, ongoing education, and proactive management of employees' projects so that they are rounding out their experience. Think executive MBA; think coding classes; think seminars or coaching sessions.

It can also include companies investing in their employees as whole people, instead of pretending that people don't have a life outside the office. For example, at some companies parents who take the allotted parental leave can still experience something that looks a lot like shaming. And so is it any surprise that so many women don't want to return to that company after their leave is over?

This is bad for a woman—for so many obvious reasons. And it is terrible for companies—that are throwing away their whole investment in this woman by disrespecting her at a key moment in her family's life. (Also, as we'll discuss later, an investment in parental leave pays off very quickly for a company.)

Who is more valuable to a company than someone they trained well? And who would you rather work for: a company that invests in you, or one that lets you fend for yourself? So if you're considering a position at a company, make sure it offers plenty of opportunities for training and professional development. Then once you're there, be sure to embrace that love of learning and take advantage of them.

4. Look at How the Company Treats Its Senior People If They Misbehave

Does the company look the other way when its top producer yells at an administrative assistant until she dissolves in tears? Yes, I've seen this happen.

Does the company say it welcomes open communication with its employees and then gives some of them canned softball questions to read during town halls? I've seen this, too.

Does the company give a division that "always makes its numbers" free rein to do whatever it takes to hit those numbers, even things that might be a bit—or more than a bit—over the line ethically? I've also seen this. (Again and again, actually. One company that was a client of mine used to turn a blind eye to their top performers' dwarf-throwing parties. That's right, dwarf-throwing parties.)

It's easy to hold a junior employee to basic ethical standards, but does your company hold the hotshot to them as well?

When the moral codes and the expected respect level are different for the guy in the mailroom versus the sales ace, that tells you a lot about a company's culture.

While the way a company treats its employees is not the full story on its values and its culture and how it engages with the world around it, I would argue that it's the proverbial canary in the coal mine. Honestly, is it a coincidence that the same big banks that have hired and fired people so rapidly also evicted so many people from their homes during the mortgage crisis?

The point is, do your homework. Talk to employees and former employees. Research the company lore. Go to new services and websites that crowdsource information on corporate culture. Do everything you can to get a handle on a company's culture, before you join it.

Once we're in a company, we all have the power to help shape its values and thus the impact they have on the world. So I would urge you to have the discussion of values in company town halls, with your boss, and with your peers. Companies need to ask more questions like, Who are we? What do we want to be? What impact do we want to have on the world? And, more specifically,

How do our corporate values guide us when we decide whether to scale back employee health benefits? Or, How do our corporate values guide us when we consider raising the price of our product? We can *all* encourage our employers to ask these questions, whether we work in the corner office or the corner cubicle.

While it might be scary, what's so exciting about this is that it can make our companies so much better. And it can be driven by our firm belief that companies can not only make money, but also have a positive impact on the world around them. It doesn't matter what position we hold or where we are on the corporate ladder.

Smart companies are beginning to initiate courageous conversations like these themselves. And I'm seeing it more and more front and center at start-ups. What I'm seeing in any number of them—Ellevest included—is that they are being very deliberate about building their cultures, not just allowing them to sort of form themselves. They are being mindful of culture from the very beginning, and they are consciously having conversations about how to shape it. How will they treat their people? What impact do they want to have on the world around them, including their communities? Will they value deliberate, thoughtful problem solving, or will they emphasize speed in making decisions? Does the shareholder come first, or the customer? Or the employees? What *is* their relationship with those employees? Do they truly value diversity or merely give it lip service? Smart companies realize that these values are worth understanding—and working to instill throughout the organization.

We can all have an impact on culture, one courageous conversation at a time.

CHAPTER 12

The Flexibility Without Shame Conversation

Among the key "courageous conversations" I believe we need to own in the workplace is one about flexibility. Real flexibility. Flexibility without shame. That means that if the HR handbook promises six weeks of maternity leave, we aren't intimated or "side-eyed" out of actually taking it. Meaning that if we have to or want to go part-time for a bit to take care of family, our commitment to the company won't be questioned and our promotion prospects won't be diminished.

I'm talking here about flexibility that recognizes that employees are real people, real people with real lives, and not some 1950s stereotype of what an ideal worker should be. I also believe that we need to internalize the truth of the matter: that being real people makes us great employees, not the opposite.

There continues to be a pretty discouraging double standard in many environments, where women feel like they have to hide their personal lives (that they have kids, may someday have kids, or simply have a full life outside of the office), whereas men can put their family lives on display without shame. Ever notice how when fathers leave early to go to their kid's baseball game, people say, "Wow, what a good dad," but when a woman does it, it's perceived as a lack of commitment to the job? And it's even worse than that: historically, a woman's salary and job opportunities have taken a hit after she has children, whereas at some companies men have received a "fatherhood bonus" in the form of a pay bump.[1]

We have the power to help build cultures in which we can be our full selves—whether that means on the home front opting to stay single or to get married or to become a mother—without shame or judgment.

Let me start with my own story to illustrate just how important this is. Some months after I had been given the boot by Bank of America, my son Johnathan graduated from high school. As I listened to him give his (IMHO funny, insightful, sharp) graduation speech, it seemed like another bittersweet ending. A summer of travel and work and then off to college. Pretty soon, if my own recollection of college was correct, visits home would be limited to major holidays and a few long weekends. I wouldn't go so far as to say that he didn't need me anymore, but the heavy lifting appeared to be over.

A few hours later, he was asleep in his bed, no doubt from the exhaustion of the last few weeks of high school and the prom. Then came the fever and some stomach pain. The excruciating headache. So a trip to the doctor, followed by a trip to the emergency room for dehydration, from which he was sent home with apple juice (ah, modern medicine).

More pain in his stomach and in his shoulder. Another trip to the doctor, diagnosed as the flu, and a prescription for Tylenol. Extra strength. A call to the doctor when the pain became significant, with further reassurances that there was no reason to worry. And instructions that if the situation worsened to "just call me in the morning." So another call. And another over the next few days.

And then I was sitting by his bed in the middle of the night, listening to my more or less grown son literally crying from the pain that the doctor said was nothing out of the ordinary for this version of the flu. I almost believed him—that is, until I thought Johnathan had fallen asleep and I got up to leave. He said, at eighteen, words I hadn't heard for at least a decade: "Mommy, please don't leave me."

It was as though I had sustained an electrical shock, as I realized that my son was very sick, regardless of what any doctor was telling me. I went into full mama bear mode, getting him out of bed and straight to a (different) emergency room, where I refused to leave until they ran every test they could think of to explain my son's pain.

Johnathan's spleen had become so swollen that it was bleeding into his belly, something that the doctors had overlooked for days (but for which shoulder pain, I soon learned, is a bull's-eye indicator). This was the result of mononucleosis, the "kissing disease" (ah, teenagers . . .), which affects many at his age to a slight degree, and a few to a significant degree. Well, he was definitely the latter. He was in the hospital on complete bed rest for the better part of a week to save his spleen, and out of commission for a full month. It took months and months for him to get back to 100 percent. I didn't leave the hospital for a single minute while he was there, and I think if I had tried, he wouldn't have allowed me to. And once he convinced us he was finally well enough to head up to school, my husband and I practically moved into the local hotel near his college to help him navigate the tough road of his recovery.

The point is, I really have no idea how I would have managed to be present in this way for Johnathan if I were still working at the bank, traveling my customary three to four days and nights a week. Frankly, I can't stand to think about it. After all, at one of my big company jobs, I'd once had a health scare myself and had

had to leave an off-site to get a brain scan. My boss's response when I told him my reason for stepping out: "Okay, hurry back as soon as you're done."

Not "Oh no, Sallie, please take the time you need." Or even, "Gosh, Sallie, I hope everything turns out okay." No, it was "Hurry back."

And lest you think I used a gentle euphemism for my absence, or lied and told him I was going out to get my hair done: no, I told him it was a *BRAIN SCAN*. (He never asked me how it turned out, either. Answer: it turned out that what I was suffering from was stress related—no surprise there!)

So, it's hard to think I could have managed my son's illness if I had still been working in that kind of inflexible (to say the least) environment. Thank goodness at that point I had transitioned to being an entrepreneur, so I could do right by my family *and* continue to have a career that I loved, navigating that time without the further worry that I might be fired at any second.

And then, once Johnathan got better, almost as soon as I found myself thinking, *Boy, having kids is tough. Can't believe that happened with Johnathan. I guess that was our "bad thing," the story of the close call we'll tell for years*—bam. Once again, lightning struck.

It was Labor Day weekend. The middle of the Saturday. I was in the kitchen shelling crabs, making a mess, when my daughter called with these ominous words: "Mommy, I'm okay." And then she burst into tears.

She had been in a car accident and, it turns out, suffered a severe concussion. She was out of school for months, was homeschooled for awhile, and the early treatment involved her lying in a dark room for hours at a time with little stimulation. And so I lay there with her. Again, I thought, it was a good thing I wasn't working for the aforementioned company at the time, because you couldn't have dragged me away from her.

Did each of these events mean I lost my desire to work? Or my ambition? Absolutely not. They were just . . . life happening.

But here's the thing, it's not just flexibility on the "big things" like this that matter. Because it isn't always the "big things" that can knock us off track. Sometimes it's an accumulation of the "little things." Add up years and years of the "little things" and suddenly they aren't quite so little.

How quickly can they add up? Well, here's one example. When I was Citigroup's chief financial officer, I took my team—which included a lot of men—down to Brazil for business reviews and client meetings. We had been out very late the night before, until after one in the morning, and were scheduled to meet in the hotel lobby very early, before 5 a.m., to catch a flight to Argentina.

When I arrived in the lobby, the guys were milling around, with the typical discussion of how tired everyone was and how little sleep everyone had gotten. The guys were all complaining and mumbling that they had just rolled out of bed.

Me? I had been awake for one hour. One solid hour.

The reason?

Hair and makeup.

"Huh?" you may say.

But I'm being serious here, so please give me a minute. Because I had an insight that morning that we often don't discuss.

Our society dictates that we professional women wear makeup. That we be well groomed. That we look "put together." Newsflash, guys. It takes time. Let's do the math:

Let's assume you're not as "high maintenance" as I am, that your hair and makeup don't take as long as mine. Let's assume you only take fifteen minutes for grooming in the morning. Well, another newsflash: that's fifteen minutes more a day than a typical guy does. (At one point, my husband tried to counter my assertion that women spend more time on grooming than men by telling me that he has to shave his face. I retorted that I have to shave my *legs*. Boom!)

Fifteen minutes a day is nothing, right? No big deal. It's just fifteen minutes.

Well, let's do some math. Because that 15 minutes a day is 1 hour and 15 minutes a week . . . is 5 hours a month . . . is 60 hours a year. Sixty hours a year.

That's the equivalent of one full workweek.

In other words, that fifteen minutes a day—that no-big-deal fifteen minutes a day—is one full workweek a year.

And I haven't even gotten to the "extracurricular": the haircut, the hair color, the waxing, the tweezing, the facial, the Pilates, the manicure, the pedicure, the blowout, the you-name-it that so many professional women undergo on the personal grooming front, some good part of which society expects of us.

My husband's other input into this insight? He says, then don't do it. Put your hair in a ponytail and go to work barefaced, he tells me.

Well, no. Because the research tells me that my looking "put together," or as some call it, having "executive presence"—the now much-discussed gravitas—is a key to my being successful in getting ahead in business. According to the Center for Talent Innovation, it may not be the most important factor, but it is "table stakes." While only 5 percent of leaders say they consider appearance a key factor in executive presence, 83 percent say unkempt attire detracts from a woman's executive presence.[2] In other words, if we don't come in looking the part—and that seems to include carefully styled hair and tasteful eye shadow—then we cede the opportunity to demonstrate our other skills and competencies.

So, the little things can add up. (And can exhaust us.)

The medium-size things add up, too: we still do much more housework than men—roughly twice as much.[3] And we still shoulder more of the childcare at home than the men do. On an average day, in a house with small children, women do an hour of physical care like feeding and bathing, whereas men spend twenty-three minutes. (I often say the smartest thing I did when my kids were small was convince my husband that when our toddler woke up in the middle of the night screaming "Mommy!" he actually meant "Parent of Either Gender!" So we took turns, and guess what. Never—during the search for the lost pacifier, or the drink of water, or checking for the monster in the closet— did little Johnathan ever say, "Uh, Daddy, I believe I requested Mommy.") And yet we women continue to shoulder these tasks disproportionately.

So those are the medium-size things.

If I'm going to be honest, in the earlier days of my career, I sort of thought we women just had to buck it up, that this was just how things were. Sure, we were going to be tired for a time, but it was nothing that a bit more hard work and a bit less sleep couldn't take care of.

But after these family health crises, my thinking changed. My conclusion is that we often don't have much of a margin for error. We've got the plates spinning, and we're fine. And then a kid gets sick and we drop one. We've got the plates spinning and then we get sick ourselves. Or we've got the plates spinning and then one of our kids struggles in school. And bam. Shards of ceramic all over the place.

Then, as we're an hour late for work because we were busy crawling around the floor picking up the broken plates, comes the double whammy. Because in general, when a woman takes time off work to deal with personal matters, suddenly the implicit assumption is that she's less "committed," or less of a "team player" (instead of being commended for putting her family first, or, as she likely would be if she were a man, for being a "good parent").

So, let me ask you a question: did the fact that I wanted (no, needed) to be with my kids when they were sick or injured make me any less committed to my career? Answer: Of course not. I promise you, I would have *much* preferred to have been working with a healthy son at school than watching my son writhe in pain in a hospital bed.

Does the fact that a woman who has a child with behavioral issues and might want to spend more time with him that first week of kindergarten mean she is less committed to her work?

Does the fact that she had a baby—and, you know, spends the first month *healing* and the next few months after that trying to make sure that child gets a healthy start—mean that she is a subpar professional?

That's what parts of corporate America can still project on us. Incredibly, today, less than a quarter of companies offer paid parental leave.[4] (Didn't they get the memo about how *hard* having a baby is?) And even those of us lucky enough to work for companies that do offer leave still hear the message that daring to take the time to which our company policy entitles us (which is usually still insufficient, by the way) makes us less committed. A McKinsey/LeanIn survey notes that 90 percent of workers believe taking extended family leave will hurt their position at work; thus just 2 percent of individuals eligible for part-time programs at US companies access them.[5]

This is certainly what the mindset was like on Wall Street when I had my children (and it still is at many companies for any number of women today). Yes, I've got a story there, too, and this is not one I'm particularly proud of. I worked up until the very end of my pregnancy: I actually spoke to clients from the delivery room. I started back at work two weeks after my daughter was born. I made my husband throw away the picture—and the negative (remember how photographs used to have negatives?)—of me nursing my daughter while working on my computer in the month after she was born. Do I wish I'd had other options to consider? Do I wish I'd had the courageous conversation about flexibility? I think you know the answer to that. And here's what I also wish: that you'll learn from my mistake and have the conversation that I didn't.

What are many women doing instead when they hit the time in their lives when they want to have kids? Today they often simply "take the hint" and leave the workforce. This is a big reason, as I've mentioned, we take career breaks averaging a total of eleven years over the course of our careers.[6]

Again, I've got nothing against career breaks when we go into them with eyes wide open. Used strategically, they can be amazing for our careers. But that's true only for the ones we take because we *want* to. What I am *not* in favor of are career breaks that are taken because our jobs do not give us the flexibility to be real people, with real lives.

Remember, career breaks have their costs for everyone. Real costs. As we noted earlier, they can cost a woman making $85,000 a year more than $1 million over the course of her career. And that's if she only takes a career break of two years and comes back to the office with a salary that is 20 percent lower than when she left. (I don't want to depress you and mention that other studies that have shown that this 20 percent reduction may be on the optimistic side—by a good bit. *The New York Times Magazine* reported that women who take time off frequently have trouble getting back to work when they want to, and in one study, only 73 percent of those trying to return to work were able to, and only 40 percent found full-time jobs.[7])

And for those who don't take a career break—and manage to "tough it out" during some hard times—what do you think lack of flexibility does to your engagement and performance? How does your quality of work look when you've been up all night with a crying infant? When you work every day for a month to make up for those three days off you took to care for a sick toddler? When you scramble to get the presentation done to catch the red-eye so you can make it home from your business trip in time for your kid's flute recital/basketball game/mock trial competition?

Not good.

And how focused do you think you'll be in that meeting you're forced to sit through while your kid is home sick and you can't be there, or your teenager gets in trouble at school and you can't get out of work in time to meet with his teacher, or your six-month-old is left in the hands of a new nanny that you had to find in a hurry on Craigslist because the one you had lined up quit with no notice?

Not very.

So it's clear that it's better for women—okay, better for *people*—when companies offer us the flexibility we need to take time off—without penalty, implicit or explicit—when our children are born, to work flexible hours when they are young and to—yes, I'm going there—miss a meeting or two to deal with family emergencies that will inevitably crop up.

But it's not *just* good for us. Which company do you think will be more successful—which will see our highest performance and attract the best talent and retain the best employees and reap the benefits of diversity? The company that has a culture that demands always-on 24/7? Or the one that allows us to be actual human beings outside of work? The company that offers paid maternity—*and* paternity—leave or the one that expects its employees to show up to work bright-eyed and bushy-tailed a week after giving birth?

And please note that when I talk about true flexibility, I'm not talking about those companies that claim to *force* their workforce to take off at least a weekend a month (fine print: the other twenty-eight days you are expected to be in the office), or the ones that make big headline-grabbing announcements like the ones some big companies have made recently about steps to "accommodate our female employees": *We'll pay for you to take your nanny on the road . . . we'll pay for you to freeze your eggs . . . we even offer on-site babysitting.*

Sounds good in theory, right? Well, we asked the women of Ellevate Network how they felt about these sorts of "perks." Sixty percent of women we polled said that they were in fact not actually helpful and just perpetuated an "always-on" workplace culture.[8] One noted (and I'm sure she's not the only one to think this) that she was sure "perks" like free "extended fertility" treatments (read: egg freezing) were well-meaning but questioned whether they implied she was now expected to hold off on having children until a more "convenient" time.

And, something very important, perks of this ilk tend to only apply to women in more white-collar, senior-level positions, where some could already afford this stuff if they wanted it.

That said, some companies really "get" the importance of true flexibility and their numbers are thankfully increasing. I remember meeting with the head of human resources at Salesforce a few years ago; she told me that in their view employees are real people and have real lives outside of work. And that the company would rather have 30 hours a week of someone's time, in which they are fully engaged at work—or 20 hours or 10 hours—rather than 60 hours or 80 hours a week of a distracted employee's time. Or, of course, none of their time . . . which is what you get when an employee can't keep it up and quits.

(It's likely not a coincidence that this same company recently ran an analysis of its gender pay gap; when the data revealed that they were paying women less than men for the same jobs, they promptly increased women's salaries by a total of $3 million to close that gap. As the CEO, Marc Benioff, later said on doing the right thing when it comes to gender equality, it is "just not that hard.")

Some executives claim that moves like these are simply too

expensive. But it's starting to become clear that that type of think-ing is too narrow. Recent research from KPMG, commissioned by Vodaphone,[9] says sixteen weeks of paid parental leave could actually *save* big companies $19 billion a year. That's right, *save.* It does this primarily by saving them the cost of finding and hiring employees to take the jobs of those who leave after having a baby.

That's a wow.

It's because by providing mothers with time to spend with their children in those early days, they enable those mothers to come back to work with confidence. As a result, the women stay in the workforce longer, and are more engaged, effective, and productive. And so they are less likely to quit. And that means the companies are less likely to have to replace them (and spend the 200 percent of an employee's annual salary that it costs to replace them).

Of course, there is a cost to these programs, but it is more than offset by the benefit, which is that parents are more likely to return after such a leave ... and be more productive at work when they are there ... and continue contributing to the company for years to come. This means they will also contribute to their 401(k)s and to Social Security, which is good for them, and good for the economy overall.

This isn't a hypothesis: we have real-life examples that prove it. California enacted a paid-family-leave policy in 2004 that enables working Californians to receive 55 percent of their salary (up to $1,104) for a maximum of six weeks. In a study of 253 employers on the effect of the policy, more than 90 percent reported either a positive or a neutral effect on profitability, turnover, and morale, according to a study by the Council of Economic Advisers.[10]

And we should note that this doesn't just help companies re-tain good talent today; it also helps attract the best talent in the future. Indeed, the up-and-coming Millennials are increasingly looking to flexibility as one of the key features of a company in which they would want to work: half of the most recent group of male MBAs say they plan to prioritize nonwork commitments over career progression.[11]

And the good news keeps piling up. Studies have shown that companies that put these types of family-friendly policies in place have stock prices that perform better in the markets . . . not over time, but the minute they announce these policies.[12]

Even if there weren't such a direct cause-and-effect, let me ask you this: At which type of company would you rather work? At a company that makes a big deal about its flexible culture, but then tells its employees to "hurry back" from a brain scan, or at a company that provides true flexibility? Which type of company do you think is going to attract the best talent? Which type of company do you think is going to be more successful in the long run? And which type of company would you like to buy from, or invest in?

I thought so.

The reasons for staying with a 1980s work culture are crumbling. Remember, we women hold more cards than ever. That means we have the power to invite our companies to join the twenty-first century when it comes to these issues. Because allowing flexibility without shame isn't just good business, it's the future.

That's why the time is ripe for a courageous conversation around this. We need to bring forward a conversation in the workplace about how flexibility without shame is good for all of us: for our companies, our shareholders, our work colleagues, our families, ourselves.

And we can enlist the guys to help us advance this conversation. Men like Mark Zuckerberg, who is leading the way on this and modeling a more complete life for the next generation of workers,[13] with his decision to take two months of parental leave after his daughter was born. Of course, not every dad is the CEO of a multibillion-dollar company, and not every dad has this option. But if more and more men take this lead and request parental leave from their employers, eventually more and more employers will be forced to get on board. The ripple effect for families will be significant. Indeed, the Institute for Labor Market Policy in Sweden estimates that a woman's future earnings increase by 7 percent for every month of parental leave her male partner takes.[14]

And while we are initiating these more "macro" discussions, it behooves us to make sure we take advantage of flexibility the right way. That means doing our research on company policies—and culture—around these issues before we join one. It means that if you burn out—even when your company or boss drives you nuts—and you have a choice in the matter, try to have the conversation, rather than just quit. The vast majority of women I talk to don't even ask for a break when they get exhausted; they don't try to negotiate flexibility. They just walk, and when they're feeling refreshed and ready to return, they don't have a game plan. So do yourself a favor, and instead of immediately throwing in the towel, have the conversation.

I advise starting these types of conversations by acknowledging the elephant in the room—that women who take advantage of flexible opportunities have historically been seen as less committed. (Remember the lesson from She Should Run: name the issue and you make it a nonissue.) Then you should note that taking time to be with a child after his birth doesn't mean we're less dedicated or somehow less tough. (As one who has been there, I can tell you, giving birth is the thing that's *tough*. Being a new mother is *tough*. Frankly, these things can make work look like child's play.) It doesn't mean we're less committed to our careers. It just means we're human.

Talk about why flexibility is good for your company, and how this will make you a better worker . . . which in turn will have value for the company. And note how other industry-leading companies handle this. Negotiate trade-offs around it (such as that you will come in a little early every Monday if Fridays you can work from home) rather than just a "yes or no" request.

As noted, smart companies will get on board . . . and they'll do it even faster if we help them.

And if they don't . . . well, it might be time to walk out the door. More on that later.

So let's have the courageous conversations to push for the policies that actually make a difference. Because flexibility—*real* flexibility—is good for us, and it's good for our companies; it's good for everybody.

CHAPTER 13

The "Hey, Larry" (or Sometimes "Hey, Nancy") Conversation

We're not done with culture yet. The "big" courageous conversations at work that we've been talking about—on topics like company values and flexibility policies and our approach to diversity—matter a lot.

So, too, do the conversations about gender issues that arise day to day. That's because each of us is socialized to traditional gender norms in some way, to some degree, and understanding it, calling attention to it, and talking about it are ways that each of us can contribute to reducing it. (If you're thinking to yourself that you're not gender biased in some way, let me assure you—you are. I promise you, we all are.) Educate yourself, look closely, knit together the details, and you will likely begin to see the differences in how the genders are treated.

An example: Not so long ago, I was negotiating an acquisition with a gentleman who not only is a self-proclaimed proponent for women in business, but has been recognized as such publicly and globally. During our negotiations, every once in a while he would say, out of the blue and with a slight sense of surprise, "You're just great to work with. Really great. A delight!"

I would thank him, tell him he was great to work with, too, and we would move on. Then some weeks later, he would make the same point, with the same sense of surprise. In my first meeting with his board of directors, I remember it coming up again: "And she's so nice! A real positive person and a pleasure to work with."

Finally, I realized why he kept saying that as though it were a major discovery: I had run big businesses, on Wall Street, and I was a woman, and so he thought I was going to be a jerk. More specifically, he likely thought I *had* to be a jerk to make it that far as a woman in a "man's world."

But I shouldn't have been surprised, because in fact I've had the same biases. My first real recognition of this was when I became director of research at Sanford Bernstein. I didn't know many other senior women in the industry at the time, so I decided to set up some meetings with other women on Wall Street. I figured it couldn't hurt to share some experiences.

First up, a senior woman at Morgan Stanley.

Now, at this time, there was no Google, so there was no googling people on the way to the meeting to see their background and what they looked like. I remember heading over to meet this woman, drawing a mental picture of her, as we typically do. I pictured a battle-ax: in my mind she was six foot three, 250 pounds, with her hair in a tight bun. Oh, and nasty—kind of like evil headmistress Agatha Trunchbull in *Matilda*.

Well, I walk in, and it turned out she was about five foot four, as big around the waist as my wrist, funny, and delightful.

As I was leaving, I told her, "I have to confess something. I'd imagined you as this huge, ugly, total bitch."

Her reply: "I thought the same thing about you."

It stopped me in my tracks.

But it was no huge shock, really. Remember the research that tells us that in most people's minds, success and likability are negatively correlated in women.[1] In other words, we tend to think that successful women are—heck, they *must* be—"bitches." And ironically, even we women ourselves think it!

The very act of sharing this observation with the other Wall Street woman—after we had finished laughing about it—made us both aware of our own biases. And it kept us from perpetuating them. That conversation really did change my outlook, though it didn't make my radar for bias foolproof by any means. One small step . . .

Consider another story. Some years later, it was promotion season, and my senior management team at Smith Barney was sitting around the table, several hours into a review of managing director candidates.

It was time to review "Mike." Mike had beaten plan. Mike was "aggressive," he "broke some eggs"; this enabled him to "get things done."

Boy, it's good to have someone who can shake things up, we noted. We need young up-and-comers like Mike at Smith Barney to keep us all on our toes. We need people who push. We certainly need people who beat their plans. And so Mike was promoted to managing director.

Next up was "Susie." Susie also "got things done," *but* she was "aggressive" and "broke some eggs." Oh, and Susie had also beaten plan.

Well, it was noted, beating plan wasn't *that* impressive, given the strong market environment. Plus, her aggressiveness meant that she sometimes rubs some people the wrong way. And, we said, it was important to us to have a collaborative culture; it was really part of who we were.

We recommended that Susie get an executive coach to smooth out her rough edges. We would reconsider her to become a managing director next year, if she made progress with her coach, got her "egg breaking" in check.

We had just described two individuals in almost identical words and with almost identical performance. We had just promoted one and essentially chastised the other. For literally the exact same behaviors.

I wish I could tell you that I was the one to immediately notice and call out what we had just done. But it wasn't me. I wish I could tell you it was my (female) head of HR. It wasn't her, either. It was actually another of my direct reports (a male), who brought it back up about ten minutes later with a "Hey, guys, I just sitting here thinking. . . . Do you realize what we just did?"

He was so right. It was a wake-up call for all of us. We reversed course and promoted them both. And we brought in an executive coach. Not for Susie, but for us . . . all of us . . . to make us more aware of these biases.

The point here is that we all have gender biases. And as this story shows, sometimes we women are even less aware of them than men. In a way, it makes sense. We think, *Hey, I'm a woman, I can't possibly be biased against women, right?* Unfortunately, this thinking doesn't always hold water.

A couple of years ago, I was seated next to a director of a very large bank at a dinner. I couldn't help myself, and so I offered some gentle barbs about how there were no women reporting to the CEO of that bank who had operating business responsibilities—sure, there were a few women in the human resources department, but in profit-and-loss business areas, not a female to be found. It was, I said, an unforced error on the part of the CEO.

"Oh, we'd love to have a woman report to the CEO in one of those jobs," this director told me, "but no women at the company want those jobs."

"Are you serious?" was my response. Now, this was a company I knew, and know, pretty well. (Okay, really well.) And so, I told the director, I could name five women right then and there who not only would want a senior job reporting to the CEO, but were indeed well qualified to hold one of those jobs.

My view: I don't think the company or this director was look-ing for an excuse not to promote a woman, but rather actually believed there were no women in the company interested in those positions. Why? What's going on here?

Well, we know that women are less likely to raise their hands for a job or a promotion. We have to be asked to run for elected office an average of six—six!—times before seriously considering it.[2] Heck, in high school, we are much less likely than guys to raise our hands to answer a question from the teacher.[3]

This lack of confidence may reveal how women can hold bi-ases even about their own qualifications, and how this under-confidence results in missed opportunities and the perception that we are somehow less ambitious. This requires its own type of courageous conversation, to make sure we're bringing out the best in everyone.

By the way, the punch line to this story? The director was a woman. A highly accomplished professional woman.

Even she had this gender blind spot, and couldn't see that the women around her were as ambitious as she was. Talking about these issues with other women can be just as hard as talking to men about them—maybe even more so, because as women many of us think we know this stuff backward and forward. But that's all the more reason to have the conversation, isn't it?

Now, if you've spent five minutes in the workplace, you know that gender bias isn't just about who gets promoted over whom, or who reports to the CEO and who does not. There are a bazillion little "microaggressions" that, when taken together, accumulat-ing over time, can make for a pretty tough working environment.

Here's another behavior that's worth being aware of: "man-splaining." For the uninitiated, "mansplaining" is the incredibly annoying habit some men have of feeling the need to explain things to women in a slow voice, and with two-syllable words—as though we are children who are not too quick on the uptake. I'm betting you have encountered this at some point in your career. I frequently did—most notably by a gentleman who was two levels down in the business I ran. And don't think it was just me who noticed it; sometimes, as a (not very funny) joke, my team would talk to me very slowly, imitating him.

I'm not alone: according to an Ellevate Network survey, nearly half of the women reported being "mansplained" to at least once a day.[4] And it's not just annoying and insulting; according to *Business Insider*,[5] "mansplaining" actually costs the US economy $200 billion a year in lost productivity. It seems like a high number, but just think of all the work you could be getting done in the time a man spends explaining (at a pace of ten words a minute) something you already know inside out.

Some reflections of unintended workplace bias are even colder than that—literally. Here's one of my favorites: offices can be like ice lockers! That's because most companies set the thermostat at a temperature intended to be comfortable for a gentleman in a suit. And, it often seems, in a three-piece wool suit. And, on some days, typically those on which it is upward of 70 degrees *outside* the office, it feels like said gentleman may also be wearing a heavy coat. The result is that so many women, in our paper-thin sleeveless dresses, feel like we risk death by hypothermia every time we go to work. I know I used to bring an extra shawl and extra socks to the office, and I would still shiver. At one Bank of America on-site, I actually wore gloves the whole time. I had to; my fingers were literally numb. And I'm not just some weirdly cold-blooded creature. I've heard from women who bring blankets to work, keep space heaters under their desks, or drink steaming hot coffee all day long just to raise their body temperature.

I first noticed this temperature thing while I was interviewing for a job with Sandy Weill. Every time I went over to his office, I would come back and tell my husband that I was so excited about the job, that I was literally shaking in the meetings. After a few visits, I realized that I wasn't just shivering because I was excited about the job; I was also freezing!

And by the way, this isn't just a comfort issue. If we were to increase the temperature in our workplaces, we would save money *and* increase productivity. Research shows that when an office is warmed up from 68 to 77 degrees, typos decline by 44 percent and productivity increases by 150 percent.[6] Plus, the US Energy Department estimates that you can save about 11 percent on power bills by raising the thermostat from 72 to 77 degrees.[7]

I'm on a roll.

Here's another, even subtler example of gender bias at work: Not so long ago, I gave a speech at a business school to about 750 graduates—let's say it was about 450 men and 300 women. As the students crossed the stage, one of the senior members of the faculty shook hands with everyone. It fell into a rhythm pretty quickly, and about 100 people in, I noticed a pattern. This individual shook every female's hand, and he shook every male's hand. And then he patted that male on the back.

I watched this for a bit, to confirm the pattern. I then whispered my finding to the (female) professor seated next to me.

"No, that's not right," she whispered back.

"Just look," I said.

And we did. It was true for the next 20, for the next 50, for the next 100 students. And by the end of the 750, almost all of the men had received the combination handshake and back pat. Of the women, just one got the back pat; all the rest, just the handshake.

A big deal?

In and of itself, no. Of course it's not. And there can be any number of reasons for it that aren't necessarily rooted in bias.

But over the course of a career, all of those (figurative and literal) withheld pats can send a message that's very clear. Men get an awful lot more subtle, beneath-the-radar support than women do (remember all that extra feedback they get?), while we women in turn can get the subtle message that we are outsiders, or simply not "part of the club."

And of course, we now know that it's not only the guys sending these messages that women somehow "don't belong" in the world of business, much less at high levels of leadership.

Whether it comes from a male or a female, subtle gender bias matters. It matters in employee engagement, it matters in recruiting the best talent, and it matters to the bottom line. It matters enough that smart companies like Facebook are providing employee training on it. It matters enough that companies like Apple are, for the first time, publicly releasing data on the demographics of the employees it hires. Many of these companies are doing it because it's the right thing to do, but also because they realize it represents a real competitive advantage. It will help them attract and retain—and get the best out of—the best people.

We can all own the solution by calling out the sexism—however subtle—that we see in our workplace, and, if we do it right, people will respect us for it. Small-scale discussions are valuable on this front. Yes, the courageous conversations at work can be the ones we have in the town halls with our CEOs present. But they're also the ones we can all have with Larry (or Nancy) in hallways or in line at the cafeteria. We can all pull someone aside after the meeting and say, "Hey, Larry, not sure if you noticed this, but you interrupted Jane repeatedly in that meeting. And you never interrupted Jim." Or "Hey, Nancy, not sure if you noticed, but that was Samantha's great idea, which you attributed to John instead."

An even more courageous conversation: "Hey, Larry, not sure if you noticed, but you've been interrupting *me* a number of times in the meetings. I would love it if you would let me get my idea out first before you pick up the thought." Or, "Hey, Larry, you keep telling me I need to get more experience in marketing to get the promotion. I've gotten it, and I'm ready for my promotion now."

I'm not saying these are easy conversations to have. Believe me, I know. But they can be effective, especially if we use facts, and even a sense of humor, whenever possible—so that these can be collaborative, rather than combative, discussions. So they can be about us collaborating to solve this issue, putting our heads together to share information, to help our companies become better. Sure, some of these conversations can be hard, but we owe it to ourselves to have them.

PART IV

Pay It Forward

We've talked about how to invest in ourselves and our workplaces, to get ourselves and other women well positioned for the changes that are afoot. But our work isn't done yet. We have the opportunity to pay it forward, to make things better for our daughters and granddaughters and for the world that they will live in. Recall that we have enormous power, both in our numbers and in our economic clout? Remember that we have the increasing power to start profitable businesses that reflect our values—and affect the kind of change we want to see in the world? Remember that we account for more than three-quarters of consumer spending? Remember that we control trillions of investable assets? Put that all together, and that's power.

And we can use that power to invest in other women on a global scale; to invest both our sweat equity and our dollars building (and investing in) businesses that get women into positions of power and support them once they're there. When we invest in women, and in companies that support women, we bring about a rare win-win-win for our families, our nation, and our planet.

CHAPTER 14

Literally Own It: Start Your Own Thing

I am so happy to get to this chapter.

It's because I believe we are entering a great age of female entrepreneurship. And it can be powerful—for us and our careers, for our families, for our economy. It can allow us to leave companies that don't value us. It can enable us to build—from scratch—the types of businesses that embody the places at which we want to work, the types of companies that have the impact we want to have in the world around us. This is a place where we can—figurative and *literally*—own it.

Back in the day, professional women had few choices in our careers: work for an established company, leave and work for another established company, or leave the workforce and head home to raise kids. If we wanted to start our own businesses, it was an enormous cost and effort: we had to draw up plans for widgets, we had to hire people for the widget assembly line, we had to build a widget factory, we had to buy or build widget machinery, we had to establish a widget distribution system, we had to spend big dollars to advertise our widgets on one of the three national TV networks.

Today? As you read in the introduction, we are seeing a convergence of forces that are making entrepreneurialism a more attainable and attractive career path than ever before, and more and more women are taking the plunge.[1]

And even more want to: 31 percent of Ellevate Network members say they have already started their own business, 28 percent plan to in the next few years, and 16 percent say it's a dream for the more distant future.[2] Certainly not a fully representative group, but the trend here is clear.

Make no mistake: starting a business is a lot of work.

But personally, I love hard work, as do so many of us. And I much prefer to pour all of that work and all of those hours into something that my team and I own (financially, yes, but also emotionally), and I know many women who feel the same way.

I firmly believe that the rise in female entrepreneurship is not coincidental. It's being enabled by technology, yes. But at its core, it's rooted in simply the fact that the qualities women bring to the workplace can also make us terrific entrepreneurs. Think about what is required to "make it" as an entrepreneur. You need to have a vision and a passion—well, we women have the "meaning and purpose" thing down. Starting businesses can be risky, so you need to manage risk well, and look around corners—check. It's also pretty darn complicated, so you need the ability to manage complexity and see things holistically—check. Building businesses that last means it's essential to focus on the long term—another check there, too. And finally, we drastically improve our chances of success if we are committed to keeping up with the pace of change and being constantly open to learning what we don't know—yup, we do that, too.

So the shifts in technology—and the resulting increases in opportunity that are afoot—simply make it easier for each of us to bring these qualities to bear and take advantage of the handful of converging forces that are ushering in this great era of female entrepreneurialism. They include:

1. The broadening recognition that start-ups with female leadership are more successful than those run by men only . . . by good measure. Some pretty significant players in the space acknowledge this; as just one example of many, First Round Capital recently reported 63 percent better performance by its companies with women leaders than those with all-male leadership teams.[3]

2. We are beginning to see a critical mass of inspiring, uber-successful female entrepreneurs leading the way and providing role models for those who aspire to follow them. Yep, women have founded and run wildly successful businesses, such as 23andMe, Rent the Runway, The RealReal, Birchbox, Spanx, Stitch Fix, Drybar, BaubleBar, Tory Burch, The Honest Company, Houzz, Lynda .com, *Huffington Post,* Hearsay Social, SoulCycle, LearnVest, The Muse, Mom Corps, Plum Alley, ClassPass, Mightybell, Stella & Dot, Etsy, Nasty Gal, wowOwow, Net-a-Porter, One Kings Lane, theSkimm . . . You get my point. And the list gets longer every day.

There's no playing by the boys' club rules for these powerful ladies. No asking permission. And they are forever banishing the concept that women's businesses are supposed to be little or cute, or limited to "women's products."

And their success is particularly resonating with women of the Millennial generation—the female leaders of the future—such that when I'm on business school and college campuses, entrepreneurialism is the topic of just about every meeting I have with female students.

3. There is a growing ecosystem supporting women entrepreneurs and women-owned businesses. The list of organizations, tailored to women, providing some combination of coaching, networking, instruction, and introduction to funding sources is growing every day; they include Astia on the West Coast, Springboard on the East Coast, EY's Entrepreneurial Winning Women initiative, and the Tory Burch Foundation. Women's networks that can provide entrepreneurs with valuable peer and business connections include my own Ellevate Network, as well as other professional women's networks, such as UPWARD (United Professional Women Accelerating Relationships & Development), Women 2.0, Levo League, and the National Association for Professional Women.

Underpinning the emergence of these organizations and the hundreds of other smaller, grassroots networks of entrepreneurial women supporting one another is a growing recognition that there are no limits to how big the proverbial pie can grow. There are no queen bees in these networks, but rather relationship-focused women who recognize that it's not just one or two or three female entrepreneurs who can be successful, as in the old days of one seat at the table for a woman in corporate America. At this table, there is pie for everyone. We can lift one another up, and achieve more together than we could alone. A strong women's entrepreneurial network also matters here, given the idiosyncratic challenges that female entrepreneurs face. And those networks are growing fast.

4. The cost of technology is coming down rapidly. This enables entrepreneurs to start businesses in ways we simply couldn't even think of a handful of years ago. Remember my example of building the Ellevest investing platform for a fraction of the more than $1 billion Merrill spent? Yeah . . . we've moved from rows of servers in our basement to cloud computing, from building all the code from scratch to using open-source and advanced software to build on others' capabilities, from investing a fortune in building all-proprietary technology to building only the differentiators and outsourcing the rest. Today we can build competitive companies on technology platforms that cost a small, small fraction of what they once did, and with capabilities that didn't even exist ten years ago. Or five years ago. Or, in some cases, even six months ago.

5. The other costs of running a business are also coming down.
Think freelancers for certain functions, instead of full-time employees. Think short-term shared workspace rentals at places like WeWork, rather than crushing long-term leases. Think outsourcing some of the HR and accounting functions. Think videoconferencing services, such as FaceTime and Google Hangouts, as opposed to the thousands of dollars in travel costs it used to require to do business "face-to-face"; think on-demand user testing instead of expensive focus groups; and think free or virtually free cloud services instead of software licenses and physical servers.

6. The social media revolution. As we talked about in chapter 2, another wall that has come down is the one separating businesses from their customers and potential customers. If you wanted to talk with customers back in the day (well, it was mostly talk *at* them, actually), it was expensive: tens (or hundreds) of thousands of dollars for a few seconds on TV, a couple of minutes on the radio, and a handful of square inches in print. Today, sure, we have to cut through some clutter, but social media allows us to engage in real conversations with our real customers—in some cases, for free—on Facebook, LinkedIn, Twitter, and so on. If we have something helpful or smart or useful to say about our companies or products, the barriers have come down for us to say it.

7. There are ever more sources of funding for women entrepreneurs. First, let's go ahead and acknowledge what's *not* working for female entrepreneurs: the traditional venture capital structure. Despite the numbers demonstrating that start-up teams that include women have *substantially* better returns than male-only ones, women-led start-ups receive only about 7 percent of venture capital dollars. (No, I didn't just say we received less than 10 percent in 1972, or 1985, or 1996, or 2005. That statistic was from 2015.)[4]

I recently had coffee with a well-known male venture capitalist who was straight with me about how it works: it's mostly males making venture investments, and they practice "pattern recognition" in funding start-ups. That means they look for what worked before, to project out what will work again. So . . . if no women have been funded, then no pattern can emerge . . . and then no women are funded . . . and still no pattern. . . . You get the picture.

So what about bringing female venture capitalists into the business to break this cycle? There are a few, and they are amazing. But venture capital is an "apprentice" business, in which senior investors mentor junior investors. And, again, this senior venture capitalist told me, the conventional wisdom is that it takes a decade or more to really learn the craft.

Talk about a learning curve. So, I guess if the industry decides today to change, we will see that change eventually . . . maybe in a decade. . . .

Luckily, other sources of funding for us are springing up, and they play to our strengths. We are seeing massive growth of crowdfunding* venues, including women-focused ones such as Plum Alley and Portfolia. And this matters: according to CircleUp, a private equity platform for consumer businesses, female founders are nine times more successful in crowdfunding than in raising capital with traditional banks, and five times more successful than with VCs. We are also more successful than men are in crowdfunding; for tech start-ups on Kickstarter, the success rate for women was 65 percent, as compared to 35 percent for men.[5] Some folks hypothesize that it's because women's presentations on these types of sites are more complete and less shoot-for-the-moon, and the amounts they look to raise are more reasonable.

But it's not just crowdfunding: there are also angel investing

---

* Crowdfunding is the practice of raising money from a large number of people, often online and often with individuals contributing small amounts.

groups focused on making early-stage investments in women-led businesses (such as Broadway Angels, Pipeline Angels, and Golden Seeds) and for-women business loans (through the Tory Burch Foundation).

Is it an even playing field? No. Would it be better if the more traditional venture capitalists "got it"? Yes. But all of these other sources of funding mean we're building real momentum, and eventually (albeit slowly), I believe, the venture capital industry will follow suit.

In addition, as my friend Gina Bianchini, founder and CEO of Mightybell, always reminds me, let's not forget the "cheapest form of capital," which is revenues. Build a great product or provide a great service, and customers buy it. Invest that revenue back in the business—it's a much more sustainable way to grow that business, with less risk.

One more thought: we're beginning to see that entrepreneurialism is no longer just for the young, but is becoming a true equal-opportunity opportunity, expanding its impact across the age spectrum. I'm increasingly seeing women "of a certain age" find that, after the kids head off to college, they have oceans of time (compared to the juggling acts of the kids' childhood years). In addition, don't forget the fact that women are living longer. And we have valuable experience. And more mature women may have savings and the financial means to take on some business risk.

So this opens the entrepreneurial wave to more than just younger women. Think Arianna Huffington and *The Huffington Post*. Think Julie Wainwright, who founded The RealReal. Think Joni Evans and her crew of women in media who founded wowOwow. Think Deborah Jackson, who founded Plum Alley. Okay, put me on the list, too, having come to entrepreneurialism in my late forties.

The impact of women starting more businesses?

1. **Success begets success.** As more of these women-run companies are successful, the bigger investing dollars will come into them.

2. **These women-run businesses will grow the economy.** And many of them will make the lives of other women better (and more fun). I sort of doubt Rent the Runway was ever going to be started by a guy. Nor was Birchbox, or Drybar. Nor was Ellevest.

3. **These businesses will also provide great places for other women (and men) to work.** That in turn gives us even more power, because the more great places there are to work, the easier it is for us to flee those companies that don't value us, don't promote us, don't offer us flexibility or equal pay—and we will leave them, in epic numbers.

Personally, I have *loved* becoming an entrepreneur. It's because I've been able to bring all the things I've learned along the way to bear on an issue that matters to me. It's because I'm constantly learning. It's because I believe what we're doing at Ellevest to close the gender investing gap can really matter and can have a long-term impact. It's because entrepreneurialism is in some ways uniquely American and drives our economy. (Okay, it's also because I have no corporate politics to navigate, which sometimes I did well and sometimes . . . not so much.)

So, entrepreneurialism is an unbelievable experience . . . but it's not for everyone. I've often said that being an entrepreneur is harder than running Merrill Lynch (and I would know!). In fact, being an entrepreneur is the only time that I have suffered from insomnia; it's the only time that I have truly lost sleep, night after night after night (and, remember, that's after having worked on Wall Street during the financial meltdown!).

Though it's not for everyone, for a lot of women entrepreneurialism can be much better than contorting themselves to fit an unyielding corporate culture; and for many the flexibility and opportunity that entrepreneurship provides is well worth those sleepless nights. Here are some questions to think through in deciding whether the switch is right for you.

First, the practical. Do you have enough money to support yourself as you get things off the ground? Despite the (overhyped) instant-millionaire stories you see in the press, most entrepreneurial successes don't happen overnight. As the founder of a start-up, I can tell you that in the early stages it's not about how much cash you can make, but about how *little* you can make and for how long. As I learned pretty quickly, early revenues are not money in the bank, because investing that cash in market research, product testing, and more can help the business be more successful; also, if you are going to be successful, the value of reinvesting that dollar back in the start-up is worth much more than the low returns you'll get from your bank. So before you make the switch, do the math and shore up the savings account. At Ellevest we recommend that you sock away up to two years of living expenses, if you're able to, to give yourself the runway you may need to get your venture off the ground, or have a "side hustle" to pay the bills.

Then there's the "dream." If you're looking to be the founder of a business, do you have an idea that you are truly passionate about? That one you talk and think about almost all the time? The one you bore your friends with? That you are jotting down thoughts on when you're sitting in a meeting about something completely different?

If you're looking to join an existing start-up, is the founder's vision one that you sign on to wholeheartedly? If not, you may want to think long and hard about taking the plunge.

There's also the soul-searching you need to do about what making the switch will actually look like on a day-to-day basis.

Are you after the idealized magazine-cover, Hollywood portrait of a start-up, or are you thinking more realistically, more long-term about what's actually involved in running a company? In your imagination, are you envisioning puttering around a brick-walled loft with foosball table and craft coffee for a few years, and then on to becoming a billionaire? Or do you really want to do the hard work it takes to build something and create something from nothing? (Our first office at Ellevest had mice. Actual mice. We needed to be passionate about what we were doing.) Are you so passionate about the idea that you're ready to invest the energy and effort to take it big? Do you have the personality it takes to lead a team, sometimes blindly, straight into the fire, or are you the type of person who prefers following the existing rulebook and receiving direction from others?

This requires being deeply honest with yourself about what motivates you and how you best operate. Do you live for the feedback in the formal year-end review? Or do you prefer the market to be your review? Would you rather your boss tell you what to do and set your deadlines for you? Or do you prefer to work on your own timeline, and on your terms? Are you a procrastinator? Or are you hopelessly driven and self-motivated? Do you secretly like to spend half the day at the watercooler complaining about your colleagues or comparing notes on last night's must-watch TV show? Or do you prefer the space to think that comes with solitary work? Are you anxious even thinking about money, or are you ready to put many of your financial cards on the table? Do you hate seeking out advice and feedback, or can you get comfortable asking everyone you know, and everyone they know, for help building something that could do something important in the world?

It takes a certain mindset to be an entrepreneur: someone who is a self-starter, passionate about a business, optimistic (some even to the point of marginally delusional), who can handle the heat and the stress. Someone who can let go of corporate trappings and pageantry and march to the beat of her own drum. Someone who, like most women, loves to learn. Because, trust me, no matter how much you think you know or how much expertise you have amassed over the years, not all of it (in some cases, not much of it) will be transferable. The learning curve is steep when you strike out as an entrepreneur.

To be successful, it helps to be ready to go "all in." Because you *will* fail; it's just a matter of what you fail at, how big the failure is, and how quickly you recover. And you will be rejected; it's just a matter of getting past the rejections. The founders of one hugely successful career planning site I know got rejected by tens of venture capital firms before getting funded. This is not unusual. Do you have the grit and persistence to push through all the nos until getting to that yes?

And are you ready to draw on everything you've built throughout your career, such as your skills and, more important, your network? Strong, high-quality networks have been shown to be one of the key differentiators of success for entrepreneurs.[6]

Not sure if you're quite ready? Then, if possible, put a toe in the water before taking the plunge. Before I dove into the deep end, I spent time with entrepreneurs, advising them both formally (as part of their advisory boards) and informally. They got access to the expertise I had built and I got to "test-drive" the idea of working outside corporate America.

Recently at Ellevate Network, we hosted a pretty prominent entrepreneur. She runs a VC-funded start-up that's gaining some real traction. In other words, she's "living the dream." Someone in the audience asked her whether it was fun to be an entrepreneur.

She paused.

Her answer? *"Fun?* No, not really."

I knew what she meant. As an entrepreneur, you can't coast. It's stressful and humbling and tough.

But did she want to go back to working for someone else? Did she long for her days growing someone else's business? Not a chance. And neither do I.

So if, after answering all these questions, you do decide that entrepreneurship is for you, buckle up and get ready for an exciting and potentially incredibly rewarding ride.

CHAPTER 15

Invest in Change . . . Money Is Power. Let's Use Ours to Do Good

I'll say it again: money is power. And we women have more and more of it. You're probably sick of my talking about the $5 trillion in investable assets we control.

But it gets even better. By 2030, two-thirds of the United States' wealth will be in the hands of women. Plus, women control $20 trillion in annual consumer spending globally,[1] and some 80 percent of consumer spending in this country. We are set to inherit 70 percent of the $40 trillion–plus in wealth transfer that will occur over the next several decades.[2] We are buying homes at a greater rate than single men.[3] According to some studies, we are on the verge of being the majority of US millionaires.[4]

Wow.

Now, that's some power. That's power not only to improve our own circumstances, but to also move the world more in a direction that benefits all of us.

And you know we want to. We've talked about women's drive to have an impact in their lives: remember that according to the Center for Talent Innovation, 90 percent of women globally report that they want to have a social impact.[5] And we're beginning to recognize that our money—donating it, spending it, investing it—can be a powerful means of doing this.

On donating it: according to Barclays,[6] women donate almost double the percent of their wealth as men do (3.5 percent, as compared to 1.8 percent). So it follows that the more money women have, the more money we donate to causes we believe in.

On spending it: here we can also exert an impact. What if, for example, we collectively decided that the Carl's Jr. commercials were not the types of images that we wanted our sons and daughters to see? (You know, the ones where the melons cover the model's breasts . . . get it? Yeah, hilarious . . .) What if we decide that these don't align with our values and so we don't want to support that company with our spending?

In the past, we had to draw conclusions about a company's values from what we could directly observe about them or what we heard about them. But this is changing: now we have access to all kinds of information about company values—or, more accurately, whether they really live up to them—at our fingertips. Take, for example, the start-up Buy Up. Out shopping and interested in how a company you are thinking of buying from treats women? Get out your phone, zero it in on the product's bar code, and the app will provide a gender diversity grade for the company. Then you can make the decision on whether you want your purchasing dollars to support them, or to go to the products of another company.

The use of big data is getting more advanced every day, so this kind of transparency is only going to increase.

So that's donating and spending. There's also investing as a means to have an impact with our money.

Most of today's investors group their money into buckets. They have their investment money, with which they hope to earn the highest risk-adjusted return, and they have their "doing good" money, which they give away every year to charitable organizations. These two pools—making money, and making an impact—are separate.

But they don't have to be. The trend of expressing one's values—social, environmental, political—by directing investment dollars is becoming more and more mainstream, driven in good part by women. The drumbeat is growing: One research report says that about half of affluent women report being interested in environmentally or socially responsible investments, as compared to just one-third of men.[7] Another study says some 77 percent of women want to invest in companies with diverse leadership teams.[8] And another found that 76 percent of women are interested in learning more about sustainable investing (and 84 percent of Millennials of both genders).[9]

And we aren't talking pocket change here. The Forum for Sustainable and Responsible Investment reports that at the beginning of 2014, US assets in socially responsible investing were $6.6 trillion, having increased 76 percent in just two years.[10] Yeah, this is starting to matter.

Perhaps even more tellingly, this is despite the fact that much of traditional Wall Street still sort of pooh-poohs this type of investing. While in one survey, 39 percent of financial advisors claimed they offered "impact investments," one in five could not even define the term and there was little agreement among the others about what it meant.[11] Investing for impact has had a history of being dismissed as a niche market, the purview of "tree-huggers" rather than serious investors. But that's changing, fast.

A confession: I, for one, used to be in this camp. In fact, over the years, I declined the opportunity for Merrill Lynch or Smith Barney to build out these types of impact investing capabilities; I believed that there was just no way that choosing a portfolio based on a company's values or its social impact could generate the kinds of return our clients expected to see. I thought investors should invest for the highest possible risk-adjusted investment return. And then, once that had been earned, they could donate some of those earnings to make an impact in an area that they cared about. I, too, believed in the "separate pool" theory—one pool for investing, one for changing the world.

But soon I began to ask, why do these things have to be mutually exclusive?

Why does investing in something that improves society, or helps the environment, or, for that matter, advances women in business have to earn subpar investment returns? The answer is that it doesn't.[12]

So we can make money *and* make an impact by investing our money in companies with missions and values we believe in; nowhere is this more true than with companies that value diversity.

Will companies with more diverse leadership teams outperform every year? Of course not. Name one stock that does. But do superior business results typically tranlsate into superior stock market returns over time? As we've seen, there are many reasons companies with more women (and particularly in leadership positions) perform better than ones where all the top brass are men. And based on what I've seen, over a reasonable period of time the good business performance that advancing women in business brings will also result in good investment returns.

Full disclosure: a couple of years ago, I became the chair of what has become the Pax Ellevate Global Women's Index Fund, a mutual fund devoted to investing only in companies truly dedicated to gender diversity—and my decision was based on exactly this thinking.

While Pax Ellevate's investment strategy—investing in the top-rated companies for advancing women, based on the percentage of women on its board of directors and its senior management team, among other factors—might initially appear to be a niche one, it actually isn't. In fact, it's based on a criterion that is fundamental to investing. When I was a research analyst, the question I was always, always, always asked by my investing clients was "Is management any good?" It came up for every company I covered, in almost every investor meeting.

My answer was typically something like, "Yes, I think so. They seem to really know their stuff." Or "Hmm, not so much. They sounded pretty shaky on that investor conference call."

Even when I tried to answer confidently, I was pretty aware that I was hardly on strong analytical ground. I was just answering based on my intuition—which may have been better than others' intuition, but was intuition nonetheless. It was not analysis.

That was because the analyses did not in fact exist at that time. And the only research I've ever seen on this fundamental question—the quality of the management—is the research on management diversity.

So this investment philosophy is not just about "doing good," but also about "doing smart." And the ripple effects can start a virtuous cycle: when our money is invested in companies with greater diversity, that diversity drives better business results, which can drive better investment returns, which give investors even more money to invest, which in turn drives more capital to companies with greater diversity. The market, in other words, rewards the investment.

And it's not just the case for gender diversity. This same thinking can work for companies with other social or environmental missions.

So it's not either/or—as in, either good investment returns *or* having an impact. In this case, it can be *and*.

So it's time we women started taking these things into our own hands, putting our money where our beliefs are, and supporting our values with our dollars. It benefits everyone.

CHAPTER 16

You Know the Kids Are Watching, Right?

Can women have it all? Can women achieve the elusive work-life balance?

No, we can't. Yes, we can . . . as long as we don't have it all at once. Yes, we can . . . if we blend our work and life, rather than balance it. No, we can't. Yes, we can if we have the right partner. No, we can't. Yes, we can if we have our children later, when we have the seniority we need. Yes, we can if we have our children earlier, when the stakes are lower.

The age-old debate rages.

And what is "having it all," anyway? It sure doesn't look the same for everybody. My sister and I, for example, made very different choices in life. I took the path you've read about; she worked part-time while her daughters were in lower and middle school and is now transitioning back to full time as they head off to college.

So . . . did I have it all? Or did she have it all? And, while we're at it, how many angels can dance on the head of a pin?

I don't know the answer to any of those questions.

What I do know: I have tried to build the best life that I could for my family and myself. I have tried to make sure that my work has been fulfilling for me. I have tried to live the values that I believe in. And I have tried to make sure that my work has had a positive impact on the world around me.

What I also know: I believe the changes that are coming to the workplace will benefit professional women. But if I had to guess, I would guess that my daughter will want to work; I might guess that my daughter will *have* to work. And in a world where the boundaries between "work" and "life" are blurring more and more each day, she may well not have the luxury of the "have it all"/"work-life balance" debate. There will be work, and there will be life, and the question won't be whether the two can coexist, but rather *how* they will coexist; the question won't be whether there can be work-life balance, but rather *what* that blending will look like.

And so I have consistently asked myself a different question than the one about having it all. I have asked myself whether I have conducted myself in a way that sets a good example for my children, whether I was being the kind of role model I would want my kids to have. That's because I know that the kids are watching my husband and me—a lot. And that they are learning from us—a lot. Believe me, even when you might not think they are watching, they are. They are watching, constantly. And they see it all.

This lesson was underscored for me by each of my children, a few years apart.

Story#1: Some years ago, right after we caught our breath from the financial crisis, I took my then-fifteen-year-old son to dinner to celebrate the end of the school year. He got to choose the restaurant; naturally, he chose a steak house.

As we were being seated, I recognized Dick Fuld. *The* Dick Fuld. The reviled former CEO of Lehman Brothers, whom I had covered as a research analyst at Bernstein. I stopped, said hello, met his daughter, and introduced my son.

As we walked to our table, I thought, *Great. A teaching moment.*

When we sat down, I said, "Honey, that was Dick Fuld and he—"

My son cut me off . . . with energy. "You don't have to tell me who Dick Fuld is. I know who Dick Fuld is! He shouldn't be at dinner; he should be in jail!"

To my utter surprise, Johnathan went on and on and on . . . about the financial crisis, about the collapse of Lehman Brothers, about his views about greed on Wall Street.

I kid you not. And these were not topics we were discussing at home, though we had certainly been living the financial crisis. I hadn't talked to him about it because I thought he was too young to "get it" or to have any interest or opinions on what was happening on Wall Street.

But apparently he did, and let's just say they were not favorable. (And they were not favorable . . . at length. The kid was on a tear.)

Uh-oh, I thought.

"Honey," I said, after he ran out of steam, "you know I work on Wall Street, don't you?"

"I know," he said. "I googled you. You're one of the good guys."

Phew. In that moment, I felt relief that my son was proud of me. I felt relief that he thought I was "one of the good guys" and hope that he, too, would grow up to be "one of the good guys."

So since then, I've found a pretty effective way to make decisions that involve right and wrong, or navigating ethical gray areas: if my kids were standing there watching, what would I do?

The second story that opened my eyes to just how much kids notice takes place during the early days of Ellevest.

My teenage daughter, Kitty, was interning at the shared office space we were then inhabiting. Not surprisingly, our "roommates" were all bright-eyed and bushy-tailed twenty-somethings and their start-ups. The space was decent enough (with the notable exception of those mice), but the rooms were so small that

I couldn't stand up without slamming into the back of our lead designer.

"I like this office," my daughter said one day.

"Really?" I said, surprised, and wondered if she was being sarcastic, or poking fun. "Don't you remember a few years ago when I had an office the size of a football field? And remember, someone appeared every day at three p.m. with cookies? Here the conference rooms are about ten square feet and not even air-conditioned."

"But you're building something," she said without a shred of sarcasm. "And it's something you believe in. You're going to make a difference."

I honestly had had no idea she had been paying that much attention to what we were doing, or to what my new professional mission was all about, but clearly she had been—and I was moved by it. Not only by the fact that she "got" what I was doing and why it was so important, but also because she understood that while the money might not be as great as it used to be, the meaning was there in spades—and that counts for a lot. I loved that she learned this lesson from me without my having to say a word.

Kids are like sponges when it comes to absorbing lessons from the behavior we parents model for them—and believe me, if you think they aren't paying attention, you're wrong. So I've always thought that rather than beating myself up over being fifteen minutes late for the basketball game or the school play, I would focus on making sure I was exhibiting the values I want my kids to grow up with—including those around diversity and gender. Instead of asking myself whether I have work-life balance, I spend more time asking myself what values and behaviors my husband and I are modeling for our kids.

So here's what I'm not going to spend any time on in this chapter: how my husband and I made our marriage work around all the long hours and constant travel my Wall Street jobs required. Like so many of you, we just did. Day by day, we just did. We promised our children that one parent would be home with them every night and one parent would be at each key school event. No guarantees on which parent. And then we just tried as hard to keep those promises and make them work. Did we always succeed? No. Did some school events get missed? Sure. Do I believe that my children suffered irreparable damage as a result? Certainly not.

And, by the way, modeling behavior and raising awareness around gender issues is just as important for our sons as for our daughters, in my opinion. Here's where I almost blew it on that front.

When the TV documentary *Misrepresentation*—about how women are portrayed in the media—aired, I couldn't wait to see it. I knew I was going to learn a lot, I knew I was going to be depressed by it, and I knew it was going to be important to me.

About a week before it was due to air, I let my daughter know when it was coming on and asked her to finish up her homework early so we could watch it together. *Great teaching moment. Great mother-daughter bonding,* I thought.

At the appointed hour, she and I camped in front of the TV, ready to learn and bond. The show started, and we were riveted.

And then in walked my son. He sat down, too, and began to watch. Moments in, he was just as riveted as we were.

That's when I realized, *Duh. It's not just important that my daughter understand these gender issues; it's also important for my son. And my husband. And every other male in my life.*

Believe you me, I corrected that mistake. . . .

The point is, many women make different choices than I did in raising children and in managing work and family. And as with most things in life, neither choice was right or wrong. Just different. One choice I made in the workplace was to be transparent about the fact that I had children, that raising them was sometimes hard and that I was doing the best I could (I've never done the stoic thing well). Nor did I really want to work at a company that made me hide that part of my life. I decided I'd be damned if I was going to hide or apologize for that part of myself in an effort to conform to the unspoken expectation that we women "leave our personal lives at home."

No, I wanted to work for a company that recognized, even respected the fact that I had a life outside work; the kind of company that didn't view that as a sign that I was any less dedicated or committed to my job. Whenever I get together with the old crowd from my days at Smith Barney, they almost always remind me of the first time they were "virtually" introduced to my family. I had been there for just a handful of weeks. I was on a national branch managers call, with about a quarter of the branch management executives on the phone—so roughly a few hundred people. And of course they were mostly male, and mostly older than I.

I was in the middle of my spiel: how glad I was to be there, the changes we were going to make. Then I was interrupted by the sound of a phone ringing in the background: mine. I paused, then apologized and told the branch managers I was afraid I needed to put their call on hold and would be right back.

In the silence, I was later told, emails starting flying. What was wrong? It must have been something awfully important for me to leave the call. Could it be the Fed? Someone from the US Treasury calling? Or was it Sandy Weill, with some urgent business issue? Would I share what was going on when I got back on the phone?

After a minute, I rejoined the call. And I did share what was happening: I explained how when I had told my children I was going to work at Smith Barney, I had told them right off the bat that it would mean longer hours and it would mean more travel. But I also promised them two things: there would be a parent home with them every night (for a time, that was more my husband than me) and they could always, always, always call me in the event of an emergency.

So, no, it was not a government regulator or the CEO on the phone. It was my daughter Kitty, six years old then, telling me she had an emergency . . . she couldn't find the pink nail polish.

I laughed; the executives laughed. Now, I could certainly have hidden this. I could easily have lied and said it was Sandy, or the Fed, or whatever. But the truth was, well, more true—and, plus, it was funny. And I honestly didn't want to work at any company that didn't appreciate the vital importance of pink nail polish to a six-year-old.

When I get together to have a couple of glasses of wine with my "squad" and we talk about how we're all managing our lives, balancing family and work, and so on, sometimes the issue of whether we will regret our choices later comes up. I don't.

How do I know? Some years ago, I was on a plane with a bunch of colleagues, flying between Moscow and Istanbul. We had just finished breakfast, and I was just taking out some papers to tuck into an hour or so of work when I saw the flight attendant open a bin on the plane and start frantically throwing blankets out of it onto the ground.

Jeesh, I thought. That woman *really* wants to find a pillow.

Less than a second later, I mused that it was no wonder she was having such a hard time finding a pillow, because this plane was so filled with smoke.

And the smoke was coming out of the vents.

And then I saw that the pilot was wearing an oxygen mask. And the other pilot was also throwing things around in the cabin.

We were at thirty-eight thousand feet—between friggin' Moscow and Istanbul—and there was a fire somewhere on the plane.

So we all jumped out of our seats and joined the crew in their frantic search for the source of the smoke, which appeared to be somewhere deep in the plane.

As you might imagine, my heart was beating; my adrenaline was pumping; all senses were on high alert. I was terrified. But during all of this, I actually paused for a second and thought, *Now that it's about over, do I feel guilty for working so hard in my career?*

My answer was no; I didn't regret it one bit. And I went back to that frantic search for the origin of the fire.

Happily, we found the source of the smoke, which was a short circuit behind the microwave. The pilot put the fire out with a fire extinguisher and we continued on our way.

After my heartbeat returned to normal (which took some time, believe you me), I asked myself why, in the life-flashing-before-my-eyes moment, when I thought about my children, I hadn't felt regret or guilt. Yes, I hated the fact that I was never going to see them again, but I didn't feel guilty. The reason, I think, was the meaning and purpose I've always made an important part of my job.

And the lessons I've been able to pass on to my children as a result.

Sure, I got some things wrong, but here's the biggie that I did *right* on raising my kids: I've let them see me work hard and succeed, and also work hard and fail. And pivot and succeed, and pivot and fail, and keep working hard, and succeed and fail again. My career hasn't been smooth sailing or a straight line, and I never hid that from them. I remember them tiptoeing into my bedroom the morning after I was booted out of Citi, to check that I was okay; I woke up to see my young daughter gently touching my face. So, yes, they've seen me fail, and they've also seen me bounce back and reinvent my career to one that has a different complexion but also has real meaning for me. All the while, the underlying lesson has been how much work goes into work and how important resilience is, demonstrated not over weeks or months, but over a lot of years.

We have the power to shape future generations by being role models for our kids and grandkids. This isn't just about us; this is about what kind of world we want to leave behind.

Finally, You Gotta Remember to Laugh

We are, of course, very fortunate to even be having this discussion about the advancement of women. We're living lives flush with opportunities that our mothers and grandmothers could only have imagined, and that so many women in different circumstances don't have. So in some ways, given how far we've come, we're "playing with house money."

I've loved every minute of my career journey (okay, maybe not every minute, but let's say more often than not). I'm so grateful every day for the opportunities I've had in my career. I like to say I was even grateful when I was fired.

But some days are less fun than others. And the way I cope is that I try to keep everything in perspective—being late to the school play isn't the end of the world; it's really not. And I work hard to keep my sense of humor.

I don't know about you, but I love a good belly laugh, the kind where you laugh so hard you gasp for air. Yes, I know "work is called work for a reason," but in most of my jobs, I've had a comfort level that allows the occasional "laugh until you cry" moment. For me, when that sense of comfort is gone, it's a key signal.

You've gotta laugh, for instance, when a man does something

so blatantly sexist he looks idiotic—like the gentleman I mentioned earlier who worked for me at Smith Barney, who would demonstrably slow his speech when he talked to me (I may have been imagining it, but I think he also used shorter words). He appeared to think that my brain didn't work very quickly.

You've gotta laugh.

Another example is from when I was new to Bank of America, running, among other things, its US Trust division. Bank of America had a new CEO at the time, and I was determined to get on his good side. So, hosting a cocktail party in his honor at my home seemed like a good idea at the time.

In addition to the who's who of our clients whom I'd invited, also in attendance that night was our family's very sweet, very thin, very ugly, (usually) very shy black cat. Yes, I know we're all supposed to think our pets are beautiful, but really, her tooth sticks out, her whiskers are crooked, her face is smushed, and there is something wrong with her eye. It doesn't fully open.

At all of the cocktail parties I've had in my home, over the years, she's been too shy to make an appearance. But apparently she was just as interested in getting to know the new CEO as I was, because just as he was delivering his words of wisdom on the state of the economy and the strength of the bank's balance sheet from the landing on our staircase, our cat made an appearance. She wandered downstairs and planted herself a few steps above him. Which meant that, if you were one of the assembled guests below watching him, you were also watching her.

That's when, with the whole party looking on, she turned her head, looked at the CEO for a bit, looked at the audience, looked back at the CEO . . . kicked up her leg . . . and began cleaning her nether regions.

He talked, she "groomed" . . . he talked some more, she "groomed" some more . . . he paused, she paused . . . he started in again, and she started in again, both with admirable gusto and stamina. He started to sweat, she kept grooming. He wiped his sweaty brow, she just kept going. Let's just say she got her nether regions good and clean. I'm not sure the CEO ever knew what happened, or why there was so much "coughing" from the assembled VIPs.

This is the part of the story where I am supposed to tell how this seemingly mortifying event turned out to have a happy ending—maybe that I "came clean" (no pun intended) to the CEO, we had a chuckle, and the experience turned us into fast friends and business allies.

Well, that didn't happen (seeing as I was soon "restructured out"), but it did end happily in one sense—in the sense that every time I think about this story, I can't help but laugh. Let's face it, the CEO was pretty pleased with himself, and the whole place was cracking up.

And not just that: every time I think about this story I'm reminded of how much I've enjoyed my journey, even when I wasn't enjoying it—in part because the real "laugh until you can't breathe" moments show up at unexpected times and in unexpected places.

I'm really grateful for that laugh, and for all the others I've shared with colleagues and friends and family over the years. We need to find those belly laughs wherever we can.

And we should feel free to laugh, because the future is certainly looking bright. There's never been a better time to be a woman, and if we do this right, this is just going to get better and better.

Remember, we have: financial power + valuable skills + more career options + more information. Combine all of these and we can own this. We can have an impact. A big impact.

But only with action. If we keep doing exactly what we were doing before . . . we'll likely stay on this same trajectory, one by no means bad, but certainly not as great as it can be.

If we women make the investments we've talked about in these pages—investing in ourselves and our careers, investing our political capital through "courageous conversations," investing our time and our dollars in our futures and in making the world the kind of place we want our daughters and granddaughters to grow up in—we can accelerate our progress.

Remember, the growing power of women isn't good for women *or* men, and it's not women *versus* men. It's good for women *and* men. And our families. And our pocketbooks. And our businesses. And our economy. It's good for all of us. So let's get out there and own our power; let's make it happen.

Acknowledgments

Sincere thanks to Ada Calhoun for her invaluable help in shaping early drafts of the manuscript, and to the team at Crown for all their efforts and enthusiasm in bringing the book to life.

Notes

Chapter 1: How the World of Work Is Changing— and Why That's Good News for Women

1. Catalyst.org Knowledge Center, "Women CEOs of the S&P 500," February 3, 2016.

2. "2015 Key Findings," 2020 Gender Diversity Index, 2020wob .com, retrieved February 6, 2016.

3. Jena McGregor, "There Are More Men Named John, Robert, William, or James Than There Are Women on Boards Altogether," *Washington Post*, February 25, 2015.

4. Rebecca Leber, "The Gender Pay Gap Is Bad. The Gender Pay Gap for Women of Color Is Even Worse," *New Republic*, April 14, 2015.

5. Global Gender Gap Report, World Economic Forum, 2015.

6. Ellevate Network poll, April 2014.

7. Research outlining these and other benefits appears in, for example, Michàlle E. Mor Barak, *Managing Diversity: Toward a Globally Inclusive Workplace* (Thousand Oaks, CA: Sage, 2005).

8. Marisa Lauri, "Diversity as a Competitive Advantage," Barrett Rose & Lee Inc., barrettrose.com, retrieved February 18, 2016.

9. "Fostering Innovation Through a Diverse Workforce," Forbes Insights, July 2011.

10. "Better Decisions Through Diversity," Kellogg Insight, October 1, 2010.

11. https://www.shrm.org/research/articles/articles/pages/0605rquart _essay.aspx.

12. Sylvia Ann Hewlett, Melinda Marshall, and Laura Sherbin, "How Diversity Can Drive Innovation," *Harvard Business Review,* December 2013; David Feitler, "The Case for Diversity Gets Even Better," *Harvard Business Review,* March 27, 2014.

13. https://publications.credit-suisse.com/tasks/render/file/index .cfm?fileid=8128F3C0-99BC-22E6-838E2A5B1E4366DF.

14. Ronald Barba, "Women Founders Outperform Men and 9 Other Industry Insights from First Round Capital," Tech.Co, July 29, 2015. The original research can be found here: http://10years .firstround.com.

15. "Women Owned Firms in the U.S.," National Women's Business Council, January 2012.

16. http://www.forbes.com/2009/08/18/brill-women-philanthropy -intelligent-investing-wealth.html.

17. Ibid.

18. Betsy Brill, "Women in Philanthropy," Forbes.com, August 18, 2009; research by Boston College's Center on Wealth and Philanthropy.

19. Jonathan Woetzel et al., "How Advancing Women's Equality Can Add $12 Trillion to Global Growth," McKinsey.com, September 2015.

20. Jonnelle Marte, "How the Pay Gap Leads to the Retirement Savings Gap," *Washington Post,* September 17, 2014.

21. Sheryl Axelrod, "The Profitability of Diversity," LinkedIn, February 16, 2016.

22. Jay Newton-Small, "How More Women on Wall Street Could Have Prevented the Financial Crisis," *Fortune,* January 5, 2016.

23. BNY Mellon, "The Value of Women in the Workforce," Womenomics Today, March 26, 2015.

24. "Having a Working Mother Is Good for You," Harvard Business School press release, May 18, 2015.

25. The National Institute on Retirement Security puts the US retirement savings deficit between $6.8 and $14 trillion. NIRSoline .org, retrieved April 13, 2016. http://www.nirsonline.org/index .php?option=com_content&task=view&id=768&Itemid=48.

26. "Deaths: Final Data for 2013," National Vital Statistics Reports, vol. 64, no. 2, February 16, 2016. This report on the cdc .gov website gives the difference in life expectancy as 4.8 years.

27. "Women Versus Men in DC Plans," Vanguard white paper, October 26, 2015.

Chapter 2: Six Things We Have Going for Us

1. Stephan B. Poulter, *The Father Factor: How Your Father's Legacy Impacts Your Career* (New York: Prometheus Books, 2006).

2. Sheen S. Levine, Evan P. Apfelbaum, Mark Bernard et al., "Ethnic Diversity Deflates Asset Bubbles," PNAS.org, October 12, 2014.

3. See research summarized here: Kira Brecht, "Are Women Better Investors Than Men?," *U.S. News & World Report*, September 15, 2015. Here's an example: Brad M. Barber and Terrance Odean, "Boys Will Be Boys: Gender, Overconfidence, and Common Stock Investment," University of California, Davis, 2001.

4. "50 Leading Women in Hedge Funds 2015," *Hedge Fund Journal*, 2015.

5. Guoli Chen, Craig Crossland, and Sterling Huang, "Female Board Representation and Corporate Acquisition Intensity," INSEAD, August 7, 2014.

6. 2009 Traffic Safety Culture Index, AAA Foundation.

7. Tomas Chamorro-Premuzic, "Why Do So Many Incompetent Men Become Leaders?," *Harvard Business Review*, August 22, 2013.

8. The study "found greater neural connectivity from front to back and within one hemisphere in males, suggesting their brains are structured to facilitate connectivity between perception and coordinated action. In contrast, in females, the wiring goes between the left and right hemispheres, suggesting that they facilitate communication between the analytical and intuition." "Brain

Connectivity Study Reveals Striking Differences Between Men and Women," Penn Medicine press release, December 2, 2013.

9. Gijsberg Stoet et al., "Are Women Better Than Men at Multi-Tasking?," BMC Psychology, October 24, 2013.

10. See, for example, Rebecca Shambaugh, "Integrated Leadership and Its Connection to Human Intelligence," shambaughleader ship.com, retrieved February 2016.

11. Dana L. Joseph and Daniel A. Newman, "Emotional Intelligence: An Integrative Meta-analysis and Cascading Model," *Journal of Applied Psychology* 95, no. 1 (January 2010): 54–78.

12. Tamas David-Barrett et al., "Women Favour Dyadic Relationships, but Men Prefer Clubs," *PLoS ONE* 10, no. 3 (March 16, 2015).

13. Mark Crowley, "How the Wrong People Get Promoted and How to Change It," *Fast Company*, April 29, 2015. Also see Gallup Report, "State of the American Manager," May 12, 2015.

14. "Q12 Meta-Analysis," Gallup Inc., 1993–98, 2006. An analysis across 199 studies, covering 152 companies, 44 industries, and 26 countries, showed profitability up 16 percent, productivity up 18 percent, customer loyalty up 12 percent, and quality up 60 percent.

15. For an analysis of what this means compared with the value of the dollar today, see Brett Arends, "Opinion: This Is Nothing like the 2000 Dot-com Bubble," MarketWatch, March 25, 2015.

16. "Short-termism and US capital markets: a compelling case for change," Aspen Institute Business & Society Program, August 2010.

17. John R. Graham, Campbell R. Harvey, and Shiva Rajgopal, "The Economic Implications of Corporate Financial Reporting," *Journal of Accounting and Economics* 40 (January 11, 2005): 3–73. They found that to avoid missing their own quarterly earnings estimates, 80 percent were willing to forgo research and development spending, and 55 percent were willing to delay promising long-term projects that met their firms' internal return-on-investment requirements. A recent McKinsey survey yielded similar results.

18. Fast Facts, "Degrees Conferred by Sex and Race," National Center for Education Statistics, retrieved April 12, 2016, https://nces.ed.gov/fastfacts/display.asp?id=72.

19. "Girls Make Higher Grades Than Boys in All School Subjects, Analysis Finds," American Psychological Association press release, April 29, 2014.

20. Ellevate Network poll, September 6, 2015.

21. Rita McGrath, "The Pace of Technology Adoption Is Speeding Up," *Harvard Business Review,* November 25, 2013.

22. "Career Capital 2014 Global Research Results," Accenture, 2014.

23. Jeanne Meister, "Job Hopping Is the New Normal for Millennials," *Forbes,* August 14, 2012. Statistics are from the Bureau of Labor Statistics.

24. Sylvia Ann Hewlett and Andrea Turner Moffitt, "Harnessing the Power of the Purse," Center for Talent Innovation, May 1, 2014.

25. Jacqueline Nelson, "Women and Wealth: The Investment Sector's New—and Crucial—Frontier," *Globe and Mail,* August 9, 2014.

26. Andrea Turner Moffitt, "What You Need to Know About Women Investors," Inc.com, June 12, 2014.

27. Ellevate Network poll, February 29, 2015.

Chapter 3: Make Sure Success Is Well Defined

1. Jill Flynn et al., "Collaboration's Hidden Tax on Women's Careers," *Harvard Business Review,* November 11, 2011.

Chapter 4: The Obligatory Ask-for-the-Raise and How-to-Negotiate Chapter (with a Twist)

1. There are many studies about this, including one in which 57 percent of male Carnegie Mellon business school graduates negotiated their starting salaries, whereas only 7 percent of the women did. Linda Babcock et al., "Nice Girls Don't Ask," *Harvard Business Review,* October 2003.

2. I project this using women-specific salary curves that include inflation from Morningstar Investment Management LLC. I add

up her annual salary amounts under both scenarios over a forty-year period and subtract the difference.

3. Maria Konnikova, "Lean Out: The Dangers for Women Who Negotiate," *New Yorker*, June 10, 2014.

4. Q&A with Linda Babcock and Sara Laschever, authors of *Women Don't Ask: Negotiation and the Gender Divide*, womendontask .com, retrieved February 16, 2016.

5. "Role of Gender in Workplace Negotiations," Columbia Business School, September 26, 2011.

Chapter 5: Out with the Queen Bee. In with New Approaches to Mentoring and Sponsorship

1. *The Jossey-Bass Reader on Educational Leadership* (Hoboken, NJ: John Wiley & Sons, 2009), 341–43.

2. Cheryl Dolan and Faith Oliver, "How to Stop 'Mean Girls' in the Workplace," *Harvard Business Review*, October 29, 2009.

3. Katherine Crowley and Kathi Elster, *Mean Girls at Work: How to Stay Professional When Things Get Personal* (New York: McGraw-Hill, 2013), lists dozens of these variations and offers suggestions for how to manage each one.

4. Workplacebullying.org/wow-bullying/.

5. Phyllis Chesler, *Women's Inhumanity to Women* (Chicago: Chicago Review Press, 2009).

6. David DeSteno, "The Funny Thing About Adversity," *New York Times*, October 16, 2015.

7. Rachel Feintzeig, "Women Penalized for Promoting Women, Study Finds," *Wall Street Journal*, July 21, 2014.

8. See Sylvia Ann Hewlett, *Forget a Mentor) Find a Sponsor* (Boston: Harvard Business Review Press, 2013), and coverage like Dan Schawbel, "Sylvia Ann Hewlett: Find a Sponsor Instead of a Mentor," Forbes.com, September 10, 2013.

Chapter 6: . . . Oh, and Some Thoughts on How to Do the Networking Thing Better, Too

1. Laura Sabattini, "Unwritten Rule: What You Don't Know Can Hurt Your Career," Catalyst.org, 2008.

Chapter 7: Career Curveballs–Why We Really Need to Get Over Our Fear of the F-Word

1. Jessica Lahey, *The Gift of Failure: How the Best Parents Learn to Let Go So Their Children Can Succeed* (New York: Harper, 2015).

2. Reshma Saujani: "Teach Girls Bravery, Not Perfections," TED Talk, February 2016.

3. Belinda Luscombe, "Why Failure Is the Key to Success for Women," *Time*, August 19, 2014.

4. "Women Leaders and Resilience: Perspectives from the C-Suite," Accenture, March 2010.

5. "Global Survey Reveals Critical Role Sports Play for Female Executives in Leadership Development and Teamwork in Business," Ernst & Young press release, June 18, 2013.

Chapter 8: How to Avoid the Career Risk You Don't Even Know You're Taking

1. Ellevate Network poll, July 25, 2014.

2. https://www.tiaa.org/public/retirement-readiness/women, retrieved February 18, 2016.

3. I project the salary with and without a career break, using a women-specific salary curve from Morningstar Investment Management LLC, that includes the impact of inflation. For the career break, I assume a two-year career break in five years, and return to a job paying 20 percent less. This is an estimate of the salary difference over the remaining career.

4. Ellevate Network poll, August 2015.

Chapter 9: The Best Career Advice No One Is Talking About

1. I project this using women-specific salary curves that include inflation from Morningstar Investment Management LLC. I add up her annual salary amounts under both scenarios over a forty-year period and subtract the difference.

2. "American Women Face Saving for Retirement 'Gender Gap' with a Lasting and Harmful Impact," BlackRock Global Investor Pulse Survey, March 5, 2015.

3. For investing, I assume an investment using a low-cost diversified portfolio of ETFs beginning at 91 percent equity and gradu-

ally becoming more conservative during the last twenty years, settling at 56 percent equity by the end of the forty-year horizon. These results are determined using a Monte Carlo simulation—a forward looking, computer-based calculation in which we run portfolios through hundreds of different economic scenarios to determine a range of possible outcomes. The lower end of the results reflects a 70 percent likelihood of achieving the amount shown or better, and the higher end reflects a 50 percent likelihood of achievement or better. Results include the impact of fees, inflation, realized capital gains, and taxes on interest.

4. "Gender and Stress," American Psychological Association, apa .org, retrieved February 19, 2016.

5. Kelley Holland, "Fighting with Your Spouse? It's Probably About This," CNBC.com, February 4, 2015.

6. See research summarized here: Kira Brecht, "Are Women Better Investors Than Men?" *U.S. News & World Report,* September 15, 2015. Here's an example: Brad M. Barber and Terrance Odean, "Boys Will Be Boys: Gender, Overconfidence, and Common Stock Investment," University of California, Davis, 2001.

7. "Think Again: Men and Women Share Cognitive Skills," American Psychological Association, August 2014.

8. "Women in Fund Management: The Report," Regender.org, retrieved February 18, 2016.

9. Nelli Oster, "Men vs. Women: Investment Decisions," Black-Rock Blog, February 26, 2014.

10. Robert Carden, "Behavioral Economics Show the Women Tend to Make Better Investments Than Men," *Washington Post,* October 11, 2013.

11. "Women Want More (in Financial Services)," Boston Consulting Group, 2009.

12. http://longtermcare.gov/the-basics/.

Part III: The Courageous Conversations

1. http://www.theatlantic.com/magazine/archive/2012/07/why-women -still-cant-have-it-all/309020/.

2. Victoria L. Brescoll and Eric Luis Uhlman, "Can an Angry Woman Get Ahead?" *Psychological Science,* August 31, 2007.

3.   "Name It. Change It.: An Examination of the Impact of Media Coverage of Women Candidates' Appearance," survey by Lake Research Partners courtesy of the Women's Media Center and She Should Run, 2010.

Chapter 10: Let's Hold a Funeral for the Diversity Council . . . and Other Well-Meaning Initiatives That No Longer Work

1.   "Women in the Workplace," LeanIn/McKinsey & Co., 2015, http://womenintheworkplace.com/#key-findings.

2.   Joanna Barsh of McKinsey, "Unlocking the Full Potential of Women in the U.S. Economy," genius.com, retrieved February 18, 2016.

3.   Dasie J. Schulz and Christine Enslin, "The Female Executive's Perspective on Career Planning and Advancement in Organizations," SagePub.com, November 23, 2014.

4.   "Women in Mostly Male Workplaces Exhibit Psychological Stress Response," Phys.org, August 24, 2015.

Chapter 11: The Company Culture Conversation

1.   "SBW Survey," Cox Business, June 2013. http://newsroom.cox.com/news-releases?item=680.

2.   Bill Barnett, "When Choosing a Job, Culture Matters," *Harvard Business Review,* May 2, 2012.

3.   Julia Rozovsky, "The Five Keys to a Successful Google Team," rework.withgoogle.com, November 17, 2015.

4.   Charles Duhigg, "Group Study: What Google Learned from Its Quest to Build the Perfect Team," an adapted excerpt from his book *Smarter Faster Better, New York Times Magazine,* February 28, 2016.

Chapter 12: The Flexibility Without Shame Conversation

1.   Claire Cain Miller, "The Motherhood Penalty vs. the Fatherhood Bonus," *New York Times,* September 6, 2014.

2.   Sylvia Ann Hewlett et al., "Executive Presence," Center for Talent Innovation, 2013.

3. "Household Activities in 2014," Bureau of Labor Statistics, bls.gov. Also see Claire Cain Miller, "How Society Pays When Women's Work Is Unpaid," *New York Times*, February 22, 2016.

4. "2015 Employee Benefits," Society for Human Resource Management.

5. "Women in the Workplace," LeanIn/McKinsey & Co., 2015, http://womenintheworkplace.com/#key-findings.

6. "Retirement Readiness Center," TIAA-Cref, tiaa-cref.org, retrieved February 18, 2016, https://www.tiaa.org/public/retirement-readiness/women.

7. Judith Warner, "The Opt-Out Generation Wants Back In," *The New York Times Magazine*, August 7, 2013.

8. Ellevate Network poll, 2015.

9. Ivana Kottasova, "Company Offers Moms 16 Weeks Off on Full Pay, Even in the U.S.," CNN.com, March 6, 2015.

10. "The Economics of Paid and Unpaid Leave," Council of Economic Advisers, whitehouse.gov, June 2014.

11. Kristen Bellstrom, "Exclusive: More than Half of MBAs Say They Will Put Family Before Career," *Fortune*, October 12, 2015.

12. Michelle M. Arthur, "Share Price Reactions to Work-Family Initiatives: An Institutional Perspective," *Academy of Management Journal* 46, no. 4 (August 2003): 497–505; Alex Edmans, "The Link Between Job Satisfaction and Firm Value, with Implications for Corporate Social Responsibility," *Academy of Management Perspectives*, August 17, 2012.

13. Matt Haber, "For Some Men, Mark Zuckerberg Is a Lifestyle Guru," *New York Times*, February 27, 2016.

14. Katrin Bennhold, "In Sweden, Men Can Have It All," *New York Times*, June 9, 2010.

Chapter 13: The "Hey, Larry" (or Sometimes "Hey, Nancy") Conversation

1. Marianne Cooper, "For Women Leaders, Likeability and Success Hardly Go Hand-in-Hand," *Harvard Business Review*, April 30, 2013.

2. Marcia G. Yerman, "Women + Politics = Change," Huffington Post.com, May 25, 2011.

3. Mary A. Lundeberg, Paul W. Fox, and Judith Punccohar, "Highly Confident but Wrong: Gender Differences and Similarities in Confidence Judgments," *Journal of Educational Psychology* 86, no. 1 (March 1994): 114–121.

4. Ellevate Network poll, February 6, 2015.

5. Shane Ferro, "America Needs to Stop Wasting Billions of Dollars on 'Mansplaining' Every Year," *Business Insider,* January 30, 2015.

6. Susan S. Lang, "Study Links Warm Offices to Fewer Typing Errors and Higher Productivity," *Cornell Chronicle,* October 19, 2004.

7. Petula Dvorak, "Frigid Offices, Freezing Women, Oblivious Men: An Air-Conditioning Investigation," *Washington Post,* July 23, 2015.

Chapter 14: Literally Own It: Start Your Own Thing

1. Carl Schramm, "Millennial Women Are Burning Out by 30 . . . and It's Great for Business," *Forbes,* November 12, 2012.

2. Ellevate Network poll, August 24, 2015.

3. "Ten Year Project," FirstRound.com, retrieved February 19, 2016.

4. http://www.fastcodesign.com/3027458/your-startup-is-more-likely-to-get-funding-if-youre-a-man.

5. Lydia Dishman, "Is Crowdfunding Leveling the Playing Field for Female Entrepreneurs?," *Fast Company,* June 29, 2015.

6. Kelsey Libert, "Your Network's Structure Matters More than Its Size," *Harvard Business Review,* February 23, 2016.

Chapter 15: Invest in Change . . . Money Is Power. Let's Use Ours to Do Good

1. Nielsen has $5–15 trillion in the United States: "U.S. Women Control the Purse Strings," Nielsen.com, April 2, 2013. The $20 trillion global number comes from Michael J. Silverstein and Kate Sayre, "The Female Economy," *Harvard Business Review,* September 2009.

2. Linda Stern, "Why Wall Street Is Wooing Women and Their Future Wealth," *Time*, July 18, 2014.

3. Susan Johnston Taylor, "More Single Women Buying Homes than Single Men," *U.S. News & World Report*, July 8, 2013.

4. Robert Frank, "How Many Women Millionaires? Depends on the Study," CNBC, July 7, 2013.

5. Sylvia Ann Hewlett and Andrea Turner Moffitt, "Harnessing the Power of the Purse," Center for Talent Innovation, May 1, 2014.

6. "Tomorrow's Philanthropist," Barclays Wealth, 2009.

7. Scott Secrest, "The Next Wave of Socially Responsible Investors Is Here," NaturalInvestments.com, November 3, 2014.

8. Hewlett and Moffitt, "Harnessing the Power of the Purse."

9. "Morgan Stanley Survey Finds Sustainable Investing Poised for Growth," MorganStanley.com, February 27, 2015.

10. Alyce Lomax, "Catch This Big Investing Wave in 2015," Fool.com, January 2, 2015.

11. Financial Advisors Respond to Client Demand for 'Impact Investing,' FinancialPoise, October 15,2015, https://www.financial poise.com/columns/financial-poise-news/financial-advisors-respond-to-client-demand-for-impact-investing/.

12. Anna Snider, "Impact Investing: The Performance Realities," ml.com, November 2015.

Index

Index